Don't Let the IRS Destroy Your Small Business

Also by Michael Savage

Good News / Bad News — A Tax Reform Guide
Everything You Always Wanted to Know About
 Taxes but Didn't Know How to Ask

Don't Let the IRS Destroy Your Small Business

▶ *Seventy-Six Mistakes to Avoid*

Michael Savage

Addison-Wesley
Reading, Massachusetts

Many of the designations used by manufacturers and sellers to distinguish their products are claimed as trademarks. Where those designations appear in this book and Addison-Wesley was aware of a trademark claim, the designations have been printed in initial capital letters.

Library of Congress Cataloging-in-Publication Data

Savage, Michael, 1946-
    Don't let the IRS destroy your small business : seventy-six mistakes to avoid / Michael Savage.
        p.   cm.
    Includes index.
    ISBN 0-201-31145-3 (alk. paper)
    1. Small business—Taxation—Law and legislation—United States—Popular works. 2. Income tax—Law and legislation—United States—Popular works. I. Title.
KF6491.Z9S28   1998
343.7305'268—dc21   97-33549
                                            CIP

Addison-Wesley is an imprint of Addison Wesley Longman, Inc.

Cover design by Thomas Tafuri/One Plus One Studio
Text design by Nighthawk Design
Set in 11½-point New Century Schoolbook by Pagesetters, Inc.

1 2 3 4 5 6 7 8 9-DOH-0201009998
First printing, December 1997

Addison-Wesley books are available at special discounts for bulk purchases in the U.S. by corporations, institutions, and other organizations. For more information, please contact the Corporate, Government, and Special Sales Department at Addison Wesley Longman, Inc., One Jacob Way, Reading, MA 01867, or call 1-800-238-9682.

Find us on the World Wide Web at
http://www.aw.com/gb/

To
M.S., B.L.S., S.J.S.
and to
Ann and Mariana

Contents

Chapter Three
Independent Contractors   **16**

Chapter Four
Salaries, Dividends, and Loans   **28**

Chapter Nine
Retirement Plans   **102**

Chapter Eleven
Owning More than One Business

Chapter Twelve
Estate Planning for Small-Business
Owners

Introduction

Who Makes the Mistakes and Why?

Small businesses are audited by the IRS more than any other group of Americans. And they get into more trouble with the IRS than any other group of Americans. Yet small-business owners are no less honest than most people. On the contrary, they are generally *more* honest. The reason for their unending problems with the IRS is that they are subject to the same overwhelming mass of tax rules and regulations that their big-business counterparts face, but they don't have the in-house staff of lawyers and accountants to deal with those problems that the big companies have. A small-business owner who travels on business or who has employees, for example, must have an "accountable plan" to document his company's travel expenses that is essentially the same plan that IBM has to have. Similarly, a small business that hires a marketing consultant must determine whether the consultant is an employee or an independent contractor; General Motors faces the same problem. But IBM and GM give these problems to attorneys who, as part of their responsibilities, analyze the IRS regulations and revenue rulings and the court decisions, then steer their companies clear of trouble. The small-business owner does not have this luxury.

In a small business, therefore, potential tax problems do not always get the attention they require. Sometimes these problems get out of control—at great cost to the business and its owners. Here are some examples of problems from actual cases that small-business owners get into:

- A Texas company willy-nilly reimburses its sales staff's traveling expenses at a flat rate of $150 per day, no questions asked. Without even realizing, it runs up a payroll tax bill of $85,000.

- A Maryland entrepreneur must write the IRS a check for $200,000 in taxes on the profits of one of his companies because, having structured his businesses incorrectly, he is unable to use the huge losses of another company to offset the profits of the first.

- A New York corporation is assessed $350,000 in taxes because the IRS has recharacterized as dividends more than half of the salaries that the corporation paid its owner-executives.

- A Florida businessman faces a tax bill of more than $500,000 because he has treated himself as an independent contractor to his own company and has set up his own pension plan, which the IRS proposes to disqualify retroactively for five years.

- A New York executive faces the loss of his Park Avenue cooperative apartment to an IRS seizure because a company he left two years earlier did not remit all of its withheld social security and income taxes.

It sounds unfair, and it is unfair. In each of these cases a successful businessperson got into deep trouble without even knowing it, and not because of bad advice. Rather, they didn't seek advice at all; and, more important, *they didn't even know that they had to*. No one is questioning their honesty, their integrity, or their business skills. They are not the problem. The law is the problem.

The Internal Revenue Code — the collection of federal tax laws — is some 3,000 pages long — in small print. Furthermore, it is interpreted by thousands of pages of IRS regulations and by literally millions of pages of legislative history, revenue rulings, private letter rulings, technical advice memoranda, and court decisions. The law often confuses even experienced tax professionals, so it is not surprising that it also trips up people whose expertise lies elsewhere.

I have written this book to help you avoid the mistakes that small-business owners keep making. It covers the seventy-six areas of the tax law that cause people the most trouble regardless of the business they are in. I have chosen the most costly problems, those that practitioners see over and over again. These seventy-six mistakes are the subjects of thousands of IRS audits and courtroom battles, testimony to the number of business owners, who, like lemmings marching to the sea, fall into the same trap:

Payroll tax liability,
Excessive salaries,
Travel and entertainment expenses,
Loans from closely held corporations,
Fringe benefits,
Forms of business organization,
Pension plans,
And more.

It is not my intention with this book to make you an expert in federal taxes, nor to examine every last tax problem that a businessperson could face, nor to provide every last solution. No one-volume work could. My purpose is not to give you all the answers (you wouldn't want to read a book that did), but to help you ask the questions, to make you stop and think: "I wonder if I'm heading for trouble here."

Any lawyer can point to at least a dozen cases in which large sums of money—in taxes and legal and accounting fees—could have been saved if only a question had been asked, a single phone call to an expert made. If this book does nothing more than make you ask a question, it will save you many times what you paid for it.

In the tax law, it is said, an ounce of prevention is worth about a million dollars of cure.

Chapter One

Interest and Penalties

MISTAKE 1
◆ **Underestimating the cost of mistakes.**

Once upon a time, the IRS charged interest on tax underpayments at the rate of 6 percent per year, simple (noncompounding) interest. At that rate of interest, it was almost good business to underpay your taxes. You could invest the tax money that you didn't pay; and since even a mediocre broker could do better than 6 percent in the stock market, you could make more money than you might eventually have to pay the IRS if you were audited. Or, if you needed money for your business, it was a lot easier (and often cheaper) to "borrow" it from the IRS than from your bank.

That was then. Today, the IRS charges interest at market rates, plus three points. The rate changes each calendar quarter, based on the market rates during the previous quarter. Since 1982, IRS interest rates have ranged from 7 to 20 percent. And there's more. Instead of charging simple interest as it did in the past, the IRS now charges interest that compounds *daily* — not annually, or monthly, but daily.

Each day, the IRS adds to your tax underpayment the interest that accrued on the underpayment on the previous day and charges you interest on the new total.

There is still more: penalties. If you (or your business) underpay your taxes for any reason other than a clerical or arithmetic error, the IRS is likely to assess penalties as well as interest. An "accuracy-related" penalty of 20 percent of the underpaid tax will be assessed under either of two circumstances: you were negligent in determining the correct tax; or you simply underpaid your taxes by more than 10 percent and the underpayment was $5,000 or more ($10,000 in the case of corporations). You can avoid this accuracy-related penalty if you are able to show a good-faith effort to comply with the tax law and some reasonable basis for taking the position on your tax return that resulted in the underpayment. More often than not, however, when there is an underpayment of tax, the IRS collects its penalties.

How expensive do mistakes get? A $10,000 tax liability that is paid three years late at a 9 percent interest rate, with penalties, comes to about $15,000. This is like paying interest at the rate of 17 percent per year, when market rates are only 9 percent. In reality, the problem is usually much worse. As a general rule, five years pass between the time a tax return is filed and an IRS adjustment to that return is actually paid. After five years, at 9 percent interest compounded daily, with penalties, your tax liability has *doubled*.

"Borrowing" from the IRS is no longer such a deal. Today, when you make a mistake on your taxes, the cost can be unacceptably high. Which is not to say that you should not try to reduce your taxes to the absolute legal minimum. On the contrary, this book is for people who strive to do that. But if things go wrong, it gets expensive. For this reason, you should know *where* things go wrong. Because usually they go wrong in the same place. To see your taxes doubled because you made the same mistake that thousands of other people made before you does not make good business sense.

Chapter Two

Employees

WITHHELD TAXES

More often than not, when the owner of a business is in serious trouble with the IRS, it's because of his employees. And usually it has something to do with payroll taxes. Payroll taxes consist of two different kinds of tax, an *employer-paid* tax and *withheld* taxes. The employer-paid tax is the employer's share of the social security tax on wages: 7.65 percent of each employee's wages up to the *wage base*, plus 1.45 percent of wages above the wage base. (The wage base was set at $68,400 for 1998, and it increases every year with inflation.)

Withheld taxes come in two versions. One is the employee's income taxes that are withheld from his paycheck each pay period. These amount to 10 to 20 percent of gross pay, depending on the number of exemptions your employee claims on his Form W-4 (more on exemptions later). The other withheld tax is the employee's share of the social security tax on wages, which is exactly the same amount of money that you, the employer, pay in social security taxes — 7.65 percent of the wage base and 1.45 percent of

wages above the wage base. The employee's share of
the social security tax is money owed the government
by the employee, but the law makes you collect it from
his paycheck and send it to the IRS on his behalf.

Combined, then, you and your employee pay a
social security tax on wages equal to 15.3 percent of
the wage base, plus 2.9 percent of wages over the
wage base. You pay half from your business, and you
withhold half from your employee's wages. And you
withhold his income taxes.

Payroll taxes get you into trouble, and withheld
payroll taxes get you into big trouble.

MISTAKE 2
 ◗ **Using withheld payroll taxes to run your
  business.**

If you have even a few employees, payroll taxes
mount quickly. After each payroll, you are left holding a large sum of money due the IRS, most of it
withheld from your employees and part of it due from
your company. You are supposed to remit these taxes
to the IRS within three days of the payroll or by the
middle of the following month, depending on the dollar amount of your payroll. If your company is short
on cash, it becomes very tempting not to remit these
taxes. You figure you will pay them after the next
payroll; after all, if you don't pay your suppliers and
other creditors there may not *be* another payroll. Of
course, after the next payroll there is another cash-
flow problem ... and, well, you didn't turn over the
payroll taxes last time and nobody said anything.

And so it goes, until the business owes the IRS more in payroll taxes (plus interest and penalties) than it can afford to pay, ever.

This is a big mistake. The IRS monitors payroll tax returns and payroll tax payments more carefully than any other tax. Eventually, and virtually without fail, it comes looking for those payroll taxes. And the bad news is that, if your business cannot pay the withheld portion of those taxes, the IRS can collect the money from you, personally, even if you run your business through a corporation.

If you operate your business without a corporation — as a sole proprietorship or through a partnership — it should be no surprise that you are personally liable for all those payroll taxes. After all, as a sole proprietor or a general partner, you have no corporation to shield you from any of your business's debts; thus, you are personally liable for *all* those debts, including payroll taxes.

When you run your business through a corporation, however, you expect to be protected from your business's debts. Unfortunately, that expectation is not met when it comes to payroll taxes. Your corporation protects you from liability for employer-paid taxes, but it does *not* protect you from the larger liability for withheld taxes. The individuals at the corporation who are responsible for remitting withheld taxes to the IRS — and that almost always means the owners — are *personally* liable for any withheld taxes that are not paid. And once the IRS concludes that it cannot collect those taxes from the business, it goes straight to the owner — to his personal bank account, to his car, even to his home — to get paid. Withheld payroll taxes are sometimes called *trust fund taxes* because the owner of the business is viewed as a trustee of the money that has been withheld from the employees. Like all trustees, if he fails to perform his fiduciary responsibilities, he is personally accountable for his mistakes.

MISTAKE 3
▶ **"If it's not my company, it's not my problem."**

Liability for withheld payroll taxes is not always limited to the owner of the company. The tax law assigns personal liability for withheld payroll taxes to each "responsible person" in a business. The term "responsible person" refers to whoever in the company has the authority to decide which creditors get paid. Often, there is more than one person who can be considered a responsible person. The owner of the company is certainly a responsible person if he is there running the business every day (and, usually, even if he is not). But the day-to-day manager of the business, or the treasurer, or the accountant, or the payroll clerk, or whoever decides which creditors to pay and when to pay them, could also be a responsible person. In other words, it is not necessary to be the owner of the business in order to be a "responsible person" who is personally liable for withheld taxes. You just have to have the authority to pay creditors. Indeed, many people have faced personal liability for the withheld payroll taxes of a company owned by someone else. In one case, the owner's $25,000-per-year secretary, who paid all the company's bills as she saw fit and who tried to help her boss by keeping the creditors at bay, was assessed with a payroll tax liability of $750,000 by the IRS because one of the bills she never paid was the withheld payroll taxes. (Her boss was also assessed.)

MISTAKE 4
▶ **Your partners will help you pay unremitted payroll taxes.**

When two or more people in a business are responsible people, the liability is *joint and several*. Each person is liable for the whole. Do not make the mistake of believing that, since you and two other people at the business are responsible people, you are liable for only one-third of the tax. The IRS can collect all of the tax from one person or part of the tax from everybody. Usually, it tries to collect *all* of the tax from *everybody,* and it stops collecting only when it has recovered all of its money. If you have two partners who are also responsible people, how you divide up the liability among yourselves is a matter between you and them, but it is of no concern to the IRS. If the IRS can collect the entire tax from you, it will do so.

MISTAKE 5
▶ **"I didn't know; therefore, I'm not liable."**

In order to be liable for withheld payroll taxes, you must not only be a responsible person, but you must also *willfully* fail to pay taxes that are due. You willfully fail to remit a payroll tax when you know that the tax is due and you choose not to pay it. If, however, other people in the business are attending to creditors and, presumably, to payroll taxes, and you do not oversee their work, you will not be considered to have willfully failed to meet payroll tax obligations and, though you may be a responsible person because you are authorized to pay creditors, you will not be liable for the tax.

This willfulness requirement, however, does not permit responsible people to turn a blind eye. If you know that the taxes are due and that they are not being paid, and if you could order that they be paid and you don't, you will probably be held liable for the taxes. Indeed, if you are the owner of the business, you usually will be obligated to *inquire* whether payroll taxes are being remitted. As an owner, you cannot delegate payroll tax responsibility to someone else and then profess ignorance if taxes are not remitted.

MISTAKE 6
▶ The revolving loan agreement from hell.

People in manufacturing or wholesale businesses frequently have revolving loan agreements with their banks. Revolving loan agreements typically operate through an account at the bank: The bank puts money into this account so that you can pay your creditors, and you deposit your customers' payments into this account so that the bank can cause the loan to be repaid. Revolving loan agreements also typically give the bank the power to control payments from this account if you default on the loan or if business starts to turn sour. Once the bank controls the account, you can pay only those creditors whom the bank lets you pay. And seldom does a revolving loan agreement state that the bank must let you pay payroll taxes.

Under a revolving loan agreement, then, a bank that has taken control of your business's account might approve the payment of the payroll—because you have to pay your employees to keep the business going—but not the payment of the payroll taxes. The bank knows that the IRS will collect those taxes from you if it has to, and so it figures that the taxes are your problem. For each payroll that the bank permits, your payroll tax exposure increases; but if you want to keep your business going, there is no way out.

To avoid this mistake, make sure to get into writing a key provision when you enter into a revolving credit agreement with a bank: Even if the bank takes over your accounts, it has to approve the payment of payroll taxes.

MISTAKE 7
◗ Failing to fight payroll tax assessments.

Many businesspeople become alarmed when the IRS attempts to collect payroll taxes from them, and they pay the taxes right away. That may not be a good idea. It is often advisable to contest a payroll tax even if you owe it, particularly if other people at the company have also been assessed for the tax. The reason is simple: By the time you are done fighting the assessment, someone else may have paid it.

Once the IRS discovers that trust-fund taxes have not been remitted, it sends a "notice of proposed assessment" to the responsible people. (The IRS calls this assessment a "penalty," but in fact the amount of the penalty is simply the amount of trust-fund taxes due.) A few things about this proposed assessment are important to understand. First, it's a *proposed* assessment, so interest hasn't yet started to accumulate. At this point, it's not costing you anything more to contest the assessment. Second, after the IRS proposes an assessment, it gives you the opportunity to demonstrate why it shouldn't actually make the assessment; it permits you to file a "protest" to the proposed assessment. And while it considers your protest — usually over several months — interest does not accumulate.

Once the IRS rejects your protest (which it usually does), it makes an actual assessment. Now interest starts to run. However, just because the IRS has made the assessment does not mean that it can collect it. It still must give you a chance to defend yourself in court. To go to court, you have to pay a small portion of the taxes due — the tax of one employee for one calendar quarter for which taxes have not been paid, even if the IRS is trying to collect the payroll taxes of 350 employees for a year. Obviously, you pay the tax for the lowest-paid employee in the company, which may come to only a few hundred dollars.

Once you have paid this small portion of the payroll taxes, you file a claim for a refund of that tax payment, which the IRS inevitably denies, and then you sue the IRS in court. If you go to court, the IRS will not collect the tax until the case is settled, and that usually takes years. (Technically, in order to stop the IRS from collecting the tax while you are in court, you must also post a bond. As a practical matter, once you file in court, the IRS ceases collection activity regardless of whether you post a bond.)

Your court case involving this one employee is a "test case." If you win your case on that one employee, you don't owe taxes for any of the employees; if you lose your case on that one employee, you owe all the taxes. However, if by the time your court case is over the IRS has collected the tax from someone else, you are off the hook. Many attorneys take their clients to court over payroll tax assessments just to give the IRS time to collect the taxes from another responsible person.

WITHHOLDING TAX EXEMPTIONS

When an employee starts to work for you, he submits a withholding exemption certificate — a Form W-4 — stating how many exemptions he is claiming for purposes of income tax withholding. The more exemptions he claims, the less income tax you withhold from his paycheck. Normally, the number of exemptions your employee claims is his problem. However, if an employee claims more than ten exemptions, then it becomes your problem. Many employers don't realize that this shift in responsibility can occur, and withholding tax exemptions have become a frequent source of trouble for people who own businesses.

MISTAKE 8
◗ **Failing to review the number of withholding tax exemptions claimed by your employees.**

If an employee submits a Form W-4 claiming more than ten exemptions, you are required to obtain the IRS's approval to withhold income taxes based on so many exemptions. The IRS fears that an employee who claims that many exemptions is intentionally causing his income taxes to be underwithheld, and it wants to verify that he is entitled to such a small withholding. Therefore, it requires you to send in the employee's Form W-4. The employee is free to send along a statement explaining why he has claimed so many exemptions. Until the IRS responds, you may withhold income taxes based on the number of exemptions claimed; but if the IRS advises you to disregard the Form W-4 because the employee has claimed too many exemptions, you must withhold income taxes based on only one exemption, or on another number of exemptions that the IRS does approve. (This procedure must also be followed if an employee who earns more than $200 per week claims to be exempt from withholding altogether.)

If you do not submit the Form W-4 to the IRS and it later turns out that underwithholding has occurred, then your company is liable for the difference between what you actually withheld and the income taxes of your employee that should have been withheld from his paycheck, based on the correct number of exemptions. For example, if you should have withheld $200 from each paycheck and you withheld only $20, you are liable for the difference of $180 per paycheck. Your company, not the employee, must pay the employee's income taxes. (This liability is not personal to you if you run your business through a corporation.)

The Tax-Protestor Victim

Your company probably won't go bankrupt if it overlooks this exemption procedure for one employee. But one company employed a group of tax protestors. The problem started when one employee mentioned over lunch that he had read that an income tax on wages was unconstitutional. The way to prevent wages from being unconstitutionally taxed, he said, was to claim twenty-five exemptions on your Form W-4 so that there would be virtually no withholding of income tax. Within a few weeks, the word was out that, for constitutional or whatever reasons, you could increase your take-home pay by about 25 percent by claiming twenty-five exemptions on your Form W-4. Approximately one dozen employees took advantage of this remarkable tax loophole. The IRS became aware of the problem about sixteen months later, when the employees started filing their tax returns. And since the employer had not obtained IRS approval for W-4 forms claiming more than ten exemptions, it received an IRS bill for more than $100,000 — the total amount of the income taxes that were not withheld, plus interest.

You Can't Get the Money Back

Can you recover from your employees the taxes that you had to pay on their behalf, perhaps by deducting the taxes from future paychecks? After all, you did pay their taxes for them. The answer is no. The tax laws prohibit you from trying to recover from your employees taxes that you were required to pay on their behalf. You are obligated to make sure that your employees don't seriously underwithhold. If you fail to do so, you are stuck with the bill.

Chapter Three

Independent Contractors

As the owner of a business, from a tax standpoint, you want everybody who works for you to be an independent contractor. If your workers are employees, you must pay social security and unemployment taxes on their wages, collect and account for withholding taxes, possibly provide health insurance and pension benefits (particularly if you wish to provide these benefits to yourself), and keep track of all these taxes and benefits. To do this requires that you conquer a mountain of paperwork. When your workers are independent contractors, on the other hand, the cost of taxes and benefits, and the paperwork, disappear. You simply pay an independent contractor what you agreed to pay him. The rest of the problems are his. He's responsible for his own social security and income taxes, and he must buy his own medical insurance and start his own pension plan.

Many employees also prefer to be independent contractors, although it is not always clear why. Probably they like not having income taxes and social security taxes withheld from their paychecks (though they still must pay all of these taxes themselves), and they may have their own pension plan (though they don't get any contributions to it from you). Also, they may have a better chance of deducting the cost of an office in their home (a subject we will return to in Chapter 7), and they may be able to claim greater amounts of travel and entertainment expenses than you would reimburse them for (see Chapter 5). If business owners and employees had their way, everybody would be an independent contractor.

The IRS sees things differently. Since the IRS can collect social security taxes and withheld income taxes more easily from the business owner than from the worker, it tends to label every worker an employee.

Unfortunately, the responsibility (and the possible cost) of the distinction rests with the business owner. If you treat someone as an independent contractor and the IRS later decides he is an employee, *YOU* are in trouble, not him. If you should have treated him as an employee, you are responsible for all the social security and income taxes that you would have paid or withheld if you had treated him as an employee in the first place. And since years may have passed since you should have collected and paid all these taxes, you will be responsible for interest that has accumulated on those amounts in the interim. For one $50,000-per-year worker, payroll taxes can amount to $20,000 per year, plus interest of another $2,000 per year. It all mounts up fast, particularly if more than one worker has questionable employment status. It is advisable, therefore, to know from the outset whether a person working for you is an employee or an independent contractor. Unfortunately, the two are not always easy to distinguish.

MISTAKE 9
▶ Treating an employee as an independent contractor.

Apart from failures to remit withheld taxes, perhaps the most frequent mistake businesses make regarding employment is treating people who work for them as independent contractors when they are actually employees.

Whether a person who works for you is an employee or an independent contractor depends on the "facts and circumstances" of each case. (Throughout the book we will discuss several "facts and circumstances" tests.) The IRS provides a number of factors that you can consider in weighing the facts and circumstances of a particular worker's employment status. No one factor is decisive, and some obviously do not apply to every situation. The factors that do apply are weighed against each other to determine whether, overall, a worker seems more like an employee or an independent contractor. As we might expect from IRS policy, these factors lean toward a finding of employee status. In order for an independent contractor relationship to be present, many of the factors must be absent.

Factors that, if present, point toward an *employer-employee relationship* include the following:

- Instructing a worker on where, when, and how to work (with the expectation that he will follow the instructions).
- Training a worker to do the job in the way that you want.

- Integrating the worker's services into business operations generally.
- Expecting the services to be rendered by a particular individual (contrasted with hiring a company to do the job).
- Providing the worker with assistants hired by you.
- Maintaining an ongoing relationship with the worker.
- Requiring the worker to devote substantially all of his working time to your business.
- Having the services performed on your premises, especially when they could be performed elsewhere.
- Requiring the worker to perform his services in a certain sequence or order.
- Requiring the worker to submit regular reports.
- Paying the worker by the hour, week, or month (as opposed to a contract price).
- Paying the worker's traveling or other business expenses.
- Providing the worker with tools and materials.
- Retaining the right to discharge the worker at any time or giving the worker the right to quit at any time without incurring a liability to you.

Factors that point toward an *independent contractor relationship* include the following:

- The person works for many people and chooses when to perform services for you.
- The worker performs services off your premises.
- The worker invests in his own facilities, such as his office or his tools.

- The worker stands to realize a profit or suffer a loss as a result of his services (for example, he has employee costs or other expenses of his own to manage or exploit).
- The worker makes his services available to the public.

With all these factors, you can often come up with almost any answer you want. But the common thread — and the one most frequently used by the courts — is the extent to which you control the result to be accomplished by the work and the means by which that result is to be accomplished. The more control you exercise, the more likely the worker will be deemed your employee.

There are as many court decisions and IRS rulings on who is an employee and who is an independent contractor as there are jobs in American business. No simple answers exist. All you can do is weigh the facts and make your own best judgment. If you are truly concerned (perhaps because you have a number of people in the same uncertain status), you can ask the IRS for your own ruling. Such a "ruling" is an opinion of counsel from the IRS on your particular problem, and its conclusions bind the IRS with respect to you. In a close case, unfortunately the IRS is likely to decide that a worker is an employee. You can also ask your tax adviser if there are any rulings or court decisions on situations similar to your own; but remember, a slight difference in facts can lead to a large difference in results.

Perhaps the best rule to follow when it comes to

independent contractors is not to make obvious mistakes. If you hire an in-house accountant, pay him a monthly salary, give him an office, expect him to work from nine to five every day, provide him with four weeks of vacation, and have him report to you every Friday morning, you can't treat him as an independent contractor merely because you *could have* hired an outside firm to do your accounting work.

MISTAKE 10
▶ **Overlooking the safe-harbor rule for independent contractors.**

The employee/independent contractor problem is not entirely bleak. Since it can be devastating to learn years later that an independent contractor should have been treated as an employee, there is a safe-harbor rule that prohibits the IRS from changing the status of an independent contractor to that of an employee *for prior years*. If you are eligible to use the safe-harbor rule, and if you meet the requirements of the safe-harbor rule, the IRS can only advise you that, in the future, you must treat designated people as employees rather than as independent contractors; it cannot collect payroll taxes from you for prior periods of service by those people. The mistake made by many small businesses is that, even though they know they may have an independent contractor problem, they don't try to meet the safe-harbor rule; or, worse, they do something that causes them to fail the safe-harbor rule.

Eligibility for the Safe-Harbor Rule

You are eligible to use the safe-harbor rule if you have a reasonable basis for treating the worker as an independent contractor in the first place. For the safe-harbor rule to be applicable, your treatment of a worker as an independent contractor must make some sense, which means it must fall under any one of three conditions:

1. Other businesses in your industry treat similar workers in the same manner as you do.
2. There are court decisions or IRS rulings that seem to support your position.
3. In the past the IRS has examined the independent contractor status of the worker in question or of other workers in a similar position and has not required a change in classification.

If you are preparing to treat one or more highly paid people as independent contractors, it's a mistake not to determine whether you are eligible for the safe-harbor rule. To do so, inquire into whether other businesses in your industry do the same thing, or whether there is some legal authority for your position. If the safe-harbor rule will not be applicable to you because there is no basis for treating a particular worker as an independent contractor, perhaps you should reconsider doing so.

Requirements of the Safe-Harbor Rule

If you are eligible to use the safe-harbor rule, to benefit from it you must also meet its requirements, which are as follows:

1. For the worker in question, you must have never treated him as an employee.
2. You must file all tax returns in a manner consistent with your treatment of the worker as an independent contractor (that is, you must file a Form 1099 reporting the money paid to him).
3. You must not have treated as an employee any other worker who does substantially the same thing as the worker in question.

For example, if you have two salespeople doing essentially the same thing and you treat only one of them as an independent contractor, you can't meet the safe-harbor rule, and you shouldn't expect to rely on it. Or, if you decide to change an employee's status to that of an independent contractor, you will be doing so without the protection of the safe-harbor rule. That is not to say that your treatment of the worker will not be upheld; but if it is not upheld, the IRS can change the worker's status retroactively, with all the expense that may mean.

If you are eligible to use the safe-harbor rule, and if you meet its requirements, then the IRS cannot recharacterize the worker's status retroactively. It can only advise you that, in its view, in the future the worker must be treated as an employee. You do not have to agree. You may challenge the IRS in court when it comes back next year to collect payroll taxes with respect to that employee, but consider yourself on notice that in the future the IRS may seek to collect those taxes from you for periods that have passed since it put you on notice.

MISTAKE 11
▶ **Failing to get proof of tax payments from not-so-independent contractors.**

As with income taxes that you failed to withhold because your employee claimed more than ten exemptions, you cannot recover from a worker whom you treated as an independent contractor the taxes you were forced to pay because it turned out that he was an employee. You end up paying his taxes. However, if you can demonstrate that he paid his own income and social security taxes, you do not have to pay those taxes a second time. You get credit for the taxes he paid (though you still must pay the employer's payroll taxes).

Demonstrating that a worker paid his own taxes is not as simple as one might think. When you try to get credit for taxes paid by your employee, one of two problems frequently arises. It may be impossible to find him, and then you cannot prove that he has paid any taxes. Or he may realize that he's entitled to a refund of half the social security taxes he paid as a self-employed person (because he was your employee and you were supposed to pay them), and become uncooperative (can't find his tax return, can't remember if he filed one). Therefore, if you are going to treat someone who might be an employee as an independent contractor, every year you should try to obtain proof from him — such as copies of his tax returns and canceled checks — that he paid his income and social security taxes.

MISTAKE 12
▸ **Treating yourself as an independent contractor to your own company.**

Many people who own corporations try to treat themselves as independent contractors to their own companies. This strategy does not work. If you own your company and work for it, you are also an employee of your company.

When the owner of a company tries to treat himself as an independent contractor, usually it is not because he is trying to avoid payroll taxes. As a self-employed independent contractor, the owner will pay the same amount of payroll tax as the company would have paid for him if he were an employee. An owner usually tries to treat himself as an independent contractor so that he can have his own pension plan and deduct contributions that he makes to that plan, or so that he can claim home-office deductions. And the IRS challenges his status as an independent contractor not to collect payroll taxes, but to deny him these pension contribution and home-office expense deductions. One owner of a company who treated himself as an independent contractor claimed nearly $1 million in deductions for contributions he made to his private pension plan over a five-year period. The IRS disallowed all of it because he was an employee, not a self-employed independent contractor; and as an employee, he could not have his own qualified pension plan.

MISTAKE 13
▶ **Letting not-so-independent contractors destroy your pension plan.**

Losing an independent contractor case can cost you more than payroll taxes; it can cost you your pension plan. In order to have a *qualified pension plan* (see Chapter 9), you normally have to cover about 70 percent of your employees. If you treated half your employees as independent contractors, and it turns out that they were employees, then your pension plan covered only half your employees. Your plan is then disqualified for all those years that you didn't cover those not-so-independent contractors. The retroactive disqualification of a pension plan has many adverse tax consequences (which I also cover in Chapter 9).

MISTAKE 14
▶ **Sticking your head in the sand over independent contractors.**

Employee/independent contractor problems can be a ticking time bomb, and you must confront them as soon as possible. With every week that passes, the problem becomes a bigger one. One landscape company had some 80 people working various jobs throughout the county. They went to work every day directly to the job site, mowing lawns and tending gardens; they received very little supervision and, as long as they got the job done, largely worked their own hours. The owner *hoped* these workers would be considered independent contractors, since he realized that he could save about $100,000 per year in social security taxes if they were. It seemed like a risk worth taking. But the IRS disagreed and, going back three years, sent him a bill for $480,000. By that time, half the people were gone so the company has no idea which of them paid his taxes on his own. Today, the pension plan for the owner and ten office workers is in serious trouble. And an expensive court battle will drag on for years; and, whatever the outcome, the owner loses. Problems like these should be addressed up front, either to get the bad news while you can still afford it, or, through planning, to turn what might have been bad news into the result that you want.

Chapter Four

Salaries, Dividends, and Loans

One of the reasons for owning a business is to spend the money you make from it on yourself. Thus, taking money out of your business at the least possible tax cost is one of the most important aspects of business ownership. It is also the area in which businesspeople and the IRS are most likely to end up in court. The stakes are high when the IRS challenges the way you take money from your business. Sometimes the IRS ends up with most of the money, and sometimes it ends up with more money than you made.

Getting money out of the business poses problems for people who own corporations. If you have a sole proprietorship or an interest in a partnership or an S corporation, it seldom matters much how you withdraw money from your business: These kinds of businesses do not pay taxes; rather, for tax purposes all of their profits flow through to you and are declared on your own tax return. When you run your business through a corporation, however, the corporation itself pays tax on its income, and you pay tax on money that you withdraw from the company. When and how you withdraw money from a corporation will determine how much tax both you and your corporation pay. If your company is successful, a failure to plan how to withdraw money from the company can be costly.

There are three ways to withdraw money from your corporation (apart from liquidating the business and withdrawing all the assets): as salary, as dividends, or as loans. Money can also be withdrawn in the form of a reimbursed business expense or a fringe benefit—methods of spending company money on yourself that we will return to in Chapters 5 and 6.

SALARIES AND DIVIDENDS

MISTAKE 15
▶ **Failing to document the reasonableness of your salary.**

From a tax standpoint, taking money from your corporation as salary, as quickly as possible, is often the most advantageous method of withdrawal, particularly if your company is profitable and does not need to retain its earnings to grow. Corporate profits that are paid to you as salary are fully deductible by the corporation and, therefore, are taxed only once (on your individual tax return). Corporate profits paid to you as dividends are not deductible by the corporation, and such profits are taxed once on the corporation's return as they are earned and again on your return when they are paid to you as dividends. Accordingly, business owners often prefer to take out most corporate profits as salary.

The IRS sees things differently. Since it can collect more taxes on corporate profits if those profits are paid out as dividends, it permits corporations to treat only "reasonable" amounts of compensation as deductible salaries. Amounts paid as salary that are in excess of what is reasonable are treated as dividends. If your corporation earns $1 million in profits, and you decide to pay all those profits to yourself as a year-end bonus fully deductible by the corporation, the IRS may come back with a different view. It may argue that only $200,000 of that bonus is a reasonable salary, and that $800,000 is a dividend. It then disallows $800,000 of the corporation's deductions for salary payments and sends the corporation a bill for about $280,000. Of course, you still pay tax personally on the full $1 million, because that income is taxable to you whether it's salary or a dividend.

You do not have to accept the IRS position; you are free to challenge it and defend your own position in court. When you challenge the IRS in court, however, you have the burden of proof: It is up to you to show that you are right and that the IRS is wrong. And it is here that even successful businesspeople realize that they are in trouble: They have not planned how they will justify a large salary, so they are unable to show that the large distribution they received ought to be treated as salary. The courts are filled with disputes over whether a corporate payment is a salary or a dividend—disputes that the IRS usually wins because the business owner cannot meet his burden of proof.

Testing for Reasonable Salary

To beat the IRS in a "reasonable compensation" case, you must first know what the law is. How is a salary determined to be reasonable? In determining whether a salary is reasonable, the courts consider a number of factors—it's another "facts and circumstances" test. The time to take these factors into account, however, is not after you have ended up in court, but when your company is paying you the salary. If you do end up in court, your case will be helped enormously if you can show that you considered these factors when you paid yourself the salary in question. The factors are as follows:

- *What are your qualifications*? Are you worth what you are paying yourself? How much experience do you have in your field? Would someone else pay you the same amount of salary? Would you pay someone with your qualifications the same amount of salary? If you can demonstrate that you considered these questions when you paid yourself that big salary, you are on the right course.
- *How hard do you work*? How many hours per day and how many days per week? What are your responsibilities? How crucial are you to the success of your company? How much do you contribute to the company, and in what areas do you make these contributions? Do you have records that document the answers to these questions? If you testify that you worked "very hard," the judge may or may not believe you. If you submit

contemporaneous time records, he has little choice but to believe you.

- *What is the size of your business, and how difficult is it to operate?* A big company in a complex business pays its executives more than a small company in a simple business.

- *What do people in similar positions in comparable businesses in the industry earn?* If your salary is in line with theirs, it is probably reasonable. If it is much higher, you should be able to explain why.

- *How much of your corporation's earnings are paid out as salaries?* How do salaries compare to distributions to shareholders? Corporations with profits are supposed to pay dividends to their shareholders; if you are the only shareholder (or if you and other employees are the only shareholders), and no dividends are being declared, you may be taking too much of the company's profits as salaries. If you are consistently taking just enough salary to reduce your company's net profits to zero, it may look as though you are trying to avoid dividend distributions. Perhaps you should make some dividend distributions to avoid a dispute over reasonable salary.

- *How does your salary compare to that of other employees in your company?* If your senior right-hand executive earns $75,000 per year and you earn $250,000 per year, your salary may be out of line. But if your business pays generous salaries to its other employees, your salary will look more reasonable. If your salary seems out of line, be able to justify it.

- *What has your salary been in the past?* If you've been making $60,000 per year for five years, and suddenly, in a good year, your salary jumps to $200,000, some of that increase may be treated as a dividend. You could avoid this result with a deferred compensation arrangement or by declaring in corporate minutes during the lean years that you were drawing a low salary in order to help the company grow and that you intended to make up for it with a larger salary once the company could afford it.
- *When during the year are salaries determined?* If you start the year with an annual salary of $60,000 and then pay yourself a year-end bonus of $200,000, it may look as though you are paying out corporate profits as salaries. If you can avoid a large year-end bonus, or justify it, you have a better chance of avoiding dividend treatment.

Having your salary treated as salary requires planning and homework. You may have to analyze your own business and your role in it, research the industry you are in, keep time records, make notes of crucial decisions that you make over the years, and more. You know that you are worth every dollar that you pay yourself, but someday you may have to persuade a tax court judge of this. It is easier to prove your case when you have prepared it along the way. If your company has made a lot of money (so that you have this problem in the first place), you probably did earn your salary through hard work, diligence, and creativity. But years after you did the work, when you are in an IRS audit or the tax court, the memory of those great ideas and long, late nights will have faded. And that is why you have to make a record as you go.

MISTAKE 16
◗ Overlooking the accumulated earnings tax.

To avoid a reasonable compensation dispute, many business owners will simply take the salary that they need to live on and leave the rest of the profits in the corporation indefinitely, particularly if the corporation is in a lower tax bracket. No excessive salary, no dividends. This approach is only of limited use, however, because a *separate* tax is imposed on earnings that are left in a corporation for no particular reason. It is called the *accumulated earnings tax*.

The accumulated earnings tax is imposed on earnings that are retained in the business but are not needed. The rate of this tax is 39.6 percent, that is, the maximum tax rate on individual income. Thus, if it turns out that you are accumulating unneeded earnings in your corporation, you have a choice: either you pay out the excess earnings as a dividend or you pay the accumulated earnings tax. Either way, you lose.

Excess Earnings

When are earnings not "needed" in the business? The answer to that question depends in part on your business. Most businesses are permitted to keep $250,000 in retained earnings without having to justify why, but companies that provide personal services in certain fields — health, law, engineering, architecture, accounting, the performing arts, consulting, and actuarial sciences — are permitted to keep only $150,000 in retained earnings without having to justify why. Once your business has retained earnings in excess of these amounts, the excess earnings are subject to a tax of 39.6 percent, unless you can show that you have a reason to retain such large amounts of earnings in the company.

Reasons for retaining earnings might be that you expect to expand your business once you have a sufficiently large reserve, or that your business needs the cash to get through downturns in business cycles, or that you are a defendant in a lawsuit. There may be other reasons that justify the accumulation of large earnings in the business, but without a reason, earnings in excess of $250,000 (or $150,000 for those aforementioned personal service companies) must be distributed to be sure that you avoid the accumulated earnings tax.

A potential accumulated earnings tax problem can often be solved in the same manner as a reasonable salary problem: by identifying as you go your reasons for accumulating earnings, and by being able to justify those reasons when the IRS comes in. If you cannot justify retaining large earnings, then you might be better off paying yourself a large salary and dealing with the reasonable compensation problem. The important thing is to determine ahead of time whether you have a stronger case for justifying a salary or for accumulating earnings, then go with your stronger case.

LOANS

MISTAKE 17
♦ Failing to treat a loan from your company as a real loan.

You can avoid taxes at the shareholder level on money that your corporation pays to you if the payment is in the form of a loan. Using loans to withdraw money from a corporation has its limitations, however. First, loans from corporations result in a *deferral* of tax, but they do not eliminate tax altogether; the day comes when you have to pay back the loan or else the IRS calls it a dividend distribution. Once you do pay it back, the money is back in the corporation, and you are faced with the problem of getting it out again. Second, your corporation does not get a deduction for a loan that it makes to you, so the money is still subject to tax at the corporate level even though it is no longer there. Loans are best utilized, therefore, if the corporation has no taxable income (because of artificial deductions or loss carryovers from other years), or if you plan to repay the loan before the corporation has to pay its taxes.

Despite these limitations on the benefits of loans, there are millions of loans outstanding from corporations to their shareholders. Each one is a potential source of dispute, because the IRS does not accept a transaction as a loan merely because you call it a loan. It will try to recast a loan as a dividend or as additional salary if it feels that a recharacterization is warranted. This is yet another facts and circumstances test, and after reasonable salary cases, probably the most common cases in tax court involve whether a corporation's loan to a shareholder is really a loan. Again, the IRS wins most of these cases because the business owner comes into court unprepared.

Whether a so-called loan will be recognized as a true loan depends on whether you intend to repay it and on whether your corporation intends to collect it. How do you show that you intend to repay a loan (or make your corporation collect it)? If you have borrowed from your own corporation, you can't simply take the witness stand and swear that you intended to repay it. The courts look for objective evidence of an expectation that the loan will be repaid — evidence, other than your own words, that suggests the required intention to repay. Here are some examples of objective evidence of intent to repay or collect a loan:

- *A note or evidence of indebtedness, or some other agreement.* This states when the loan is to be repaid and what interest rate is to be charged, and is the *minimum* objective evidence required to prove a loan. Standing alone, it will not usually win a case, but it is an essential starting point. Oddly, most shareholders in shareholder loan cases never execute a note — although you can go to a stationery store and buy a form of promissory note for about $1 which takes about ninety seconds to fill out.

- *Consistent treatment on the corporation's books.* Your corporation's books should carry the advance to you as a loan. Many business owners hesitate to do this, because an asset consisting of a receivable from the owner is not a strong one on the books and makes your financial statement look weaker, which will make it more difficult to borrow money from a bank. Also, suppliers who see a receivable from you may get scared into thinking that you will never repay the loan if the company gets into trouble. However, if you call an advance a loan for tax purposes but don't carry it as a loan on your company's books, the IRS will exploit this inconsistency. If it wasn't a loan for financial statement purposes, the IRS will argue, why should it be a loan for tax purposes?

- *Collateral or other security for the loan.* You might pledge some stock that you own, or your car, or other assets that your corporation could foreclose on if you fail to repay the loan.

- *A formal resolution by the corporation, authorizing the loan.* This makes it look as though you gave some consideration to the nature of the transaction at the time that it occurred, and decided to make it a loan. Too often, businesspeople simply write themselves a check, thinking that later on they will decide what to call the payment. And then they fail to make that decision until the tax return is prepared, if then.

- *Actual repayment in a regular, timely manner.* This goes far toward establishing that a loan is a loan. It will be two or three years after borrowing occurs before the IRS audits the corporation and asks questions about the loan, and by then you will have had a chance to repay some or all of it. If you have repaid at least some of it, you have developed strong evidence that the transaction was, in fact, a loan.

The courts will consider other factors, too, in deciding whether a payment from your corporation is a loan. Has your salary decreased by approximately the same amount as the loan? If so, that loan may actually be a salary payment. If more than one shareholder is borrowing from the corporation, and their loans are in proportion to their stock ownership, it may be that you are masking taxable dividend distributions as tax-free loans. Was your corporation in a financial position to make a loan to you? While even weak corporations must pay salaries, they don't usually go around making risky loans. This is another question for the court: Are you the kind of person to whom somebody should be making a loan? If you couldn't get a loan at a bank, the IRS may wonder, why would your corporation make one to you?

You should take all of these factors into account at the time that your corporation lends you money; doing so is likely to make your loan a defensible one if the IRS challenges it.

MISTAKE 18
▶ **Failing to charge yourself adequate interest for a loan from your company.**

Your corporation is not required to charge you interest for a loan, but the loan is more likely to be treated as a loan if the corporation does charge you interest.

No particular rate of interest is required, but, again, the loan looks more like a real loan if a *market rate* is charged. (A market rate of interest, for tax purposes, is a rate based on commercial loan transactions at the time that you make the loan. The IRS computes the market rate of interest every month, and if you use the IRS-published rate for that month, you are safe.)

Imputed Interest

Apart from the fact that charging a market rate of interest helps to sustain the validity of your loan, there are other tax consequences if interest is not charged or if it is charged at a below-market rate.

When you borrow money from your corporation and don't pay interest at a market rate, the IRS pretends that interest *was* in fact charged at the market rate, and the tax consequences are adjusted accordingly. Interest is said to be "imputed" to the transaction. That means that the IRS pretends that you paid your corporation more in interest than you actually did pay it. The IRS also pretends that the corporation paid you the money that you would have used to pay the corporation the extra interest that the IRS pretends you paid the corporation.

This Alice-in-Wonderland concept of imputed interest is best understood with an example. Suppose your corporation charges you 6 percent interest for a $10,000 loan, when the going rate is 8 percent. Although you pay your corporation $600 in interest for the year, under the imputed interest rule the IRS will pretend that you paid your corporation $800 in interest. The corporation's interest income from the loan for the year is therefore $800, even though it received only $600 from you. It is said that $200 of interest is imputed to the corporation. In addition, the IRS will pretend that your corporation made a payment to you of enough money to enable you to pay it the imputed interest. So in this example, the IRS pretends that your corporation paid you $200, which you then returned to the corporation as an additional interest payment.

What *is* that $200 that your corporation supposedly paid to you? (Here is where the trouble starts.) It is a corporate distribution to you, and, if your corporation has earnings, it is taxable to you as ordinary income. Do you care? That depends on whether you can claim a deduction for the additional $200 in imputed interest which the IRS pretends you paid to your corporation. If you can deduct the imputed interest, then you don't care because the extra $200 in income is offset by the extra $200 deduction. But the interest may not be deductible. It is not deductible if, for example, you used the proceeds of the loan for nonbusiness or noninvestment purposes (see Chapter 8). If the interest is not deductible, you have additional net income of $200 from the money you are deemed to have received from your corporation to pay the deemed additional interest.

The corporation will pay more tax as well, because of the imputed interest rule. The corporation has $200 in additional income that it never actually received. Does it have an offsetting deduction? No, because corporations cannot claim a deduction for dividend distributions.

Interest income imputed to a transaction is not necessarily a financial setback. In terms of cash flow, it's probably better to pay a tax on the imputed income than to actually pay the market interest. In the preceding example, if the $200 in imputed income is taxable to you (because you cannot claim an offsetting interest-paid deduction), then you owe the IRS additional tax of $60 (assuming an average tax rate of 30 percent). From a cash-flow standpoint, that is less costly than actually paying your corporation an additional $200 in interest. On the other hand, if cash flow were not a determining factor, you might prefer to pay your own corporation $200 rather than pay the IRS $60. The choice is an economic one. You just need to know that if you don't pay your corporation interest at the going rate, the imputed interest rules will apply, and you will have imaginary income, and you may have to pay tax on that income. If the numbers are large, you'll want to understand the consequences when you *make* the loan, not later when the IRS comes in to audit it.

MISTAKE 19
◆ **Putting too much capital (and not enough debt) into your company.**

Another way to get money out of your company tax-free is to have it repay a loan to you (instead of you borrowing money from it). The repayment to you of money you loaned to your corporation is tax-free to you. But in order for the company to repay a loan to you, you must have loaned it money in the first place. Many businesspeople make the mistake of transferring money to their companies without considering what to call the transfer. If the transfer is a loan, the company can repay it to you tax-free; it can also pay you interest on the loan, interest that, happily, is deductible by the company but is not subject to social security taxes. If the transfer is a capital contribution to the company, you can recover it tax-free only if the company has no undistributed earnings. (Through the miracles of accounting, a company can have undistributed earnings even if it has no cash to distribute.) So when you set up your company or furnish it with additional funds, it's important to determine whether some of the money you put into the company should be treated as a loan (the IRS won't let you treat all of it as a loan) and, if so, to take the steps outlined here to be sure that, years later, you can prove that it was a loan.

Chapter Five

Travel and Entertainment Expenses

A few years ago many business owners woke up to discover that the IRS was assessing payroll taxes on the money they had given to their employees (including themselves) for their travel and entertainment expenses. It was quite a surprise. For decades, businesses had given their top employees liberal expense accounts and had required little or no proof that the money was actually spent, let alone spent for a remotely business-related purpose. For many businesses, the expense account was simply a means of rewarding good employees off the payroll.

From a tax standpoint, expense account money was deductible by the business however it was spent. It was a travel or entertainment expense if the employee actually spent the money on the business, or additional compensation to the employee if he didn't spend the money on the business. If there were tax consequences, they were essentially the employee's problems: If he were audited by the IRS, he would have to prove the business purpose of the expenses that he had deducted; otherwise, he would be taxed on the expense account money that he had received. But since the expense account money was not reported as wages on a W-2 form by the employer, the likelihood of an audit was no greater than usual.

Today, all that has changed. Now business owners must participate in the process of documenting the travel and entertainment expenses of their employees. If they don't participate, the IRS always treats the expense account money as wages. Treated as wages, the money is subject to payroll tax contributions by the business and to income tax and social security tax withholding (see Chapter 2). If the business has not paid or collected all those taxes along the way, the tax bill that arrives after an audit of several years of expense accounts can be substantial.

Things have also changed for the employee who receives an expense account. Once upon a time, he could deduct all of his reimbursed business expenses, regardless of whether he itemized deductions — a so-called above-the-line deduction. More important, all of his travel expenses could be deducted above-the-line even if they weren't reimbursed. Today, no expense can be deducted above-the-line unless it is reimbursed. And even if it is, no expense can be deducted above-the-line unless it is reimbursed under a system of documentation in which the employer participates.

An employee's ability to deduct a business expense above-the-line is important to him. If he does not itemize deductions, he will lose the deduction altogether. Even if he does itemize deductions, business expenses as itemized deductions are deductible only to the extent that they exceed 2 percent of adjusted gross income. If adjusted gross income is high enough, large amounts of business expense deductions will be lost under this 2 percent formula. Nonetheless, any business expense reimbursement that the employee receives will still be included in his gross income, so he may end up being taxed on the reimbursements without being able to deduct the corresponding expenses.

Reimbursing business expenses under a documentation system in which the employer participates is, therefore, beneficial to both you, the employer, and to your employees. (Remember that you may be an employee of your own business.) This documentation system in which the employer participates is called an *accountable plan*, and it is a source of considerable trouble.

The accountable plan rules require you to reimburse employee business expenses under an arrangement that meets three requirements: the *business connection requirement*, the *substantiation requirement*, and the *return requirement*. As a general rule, if a reimbursement of an employee expense doesn't meet all three of these requirements, it is taxable as wages.

MISTAKE 20
◆ Reimbursing expenses that are not deductible above-the-line.

The first requirement of an accountable plan, the business connection requirement, is that the employer reimburse only bona fide business-related expenses that are deductible above-the-line. Which business expenses are deductible above-the-line? Most expenses that your employee incurs for your business are deductible above-the-line. For example, if your employee rents a television monitor to make a sales presentation, that expense is an above-the-line deduction. Or if he buys a part to fix equipment that a customer bought from you, that expense is an above-the-line deduction. Or — and this expense is the important one that we will return to shortly — if your employee incurs expenses while traveling on business away from home, those expenses are deductible above-the-line. You can reimburse all such expenses under the accountable plan rules, and the reimbursement is not a wage payment.

Notice I said that most employee business expenses are deductible above-the-line. Not all of them are. Some are deductible only as itemized deductions. The cost of trade journal subscriptions or memberships in professional societies, for example, are not deductible above-the-line. If your employee spends his own money on such business-related items, he can claim a deduction for those expenses, but only as itemized deductions. If you reimburse him for those expenses, the reimbursement is not made under the accountable plan rules, and reimbursements for such expenses are treated as wages.

MISTAKE 21
♦ **Failing to distinguish between reimbursements of bona fide business expenses and nonbusiness expenses.**

The business connection rule also requires that you reimburse only "bona fide" business expenses of your employees. You might ask, "What else would I reimburse my employees for?" but the business connection rule requires you to reimburse bona fide business expenses within the meaning of the tax laws, which may or may not resemble real-world business expenses. In most cases, the business connection of an expense is evident — the rented television monitor, for example — but the accountable plan rules, while they cover the rented television monitor, are really aimed at travel and entertainment expenses. With travel and entertainment expenses, the bona fides of the expense may not be so readily apparent.

Establishing a Business Connection to Travel Expenses

An example of a business expense that would not usually be considered a bona fide business expense under the tax laws is the payment of the travel cost of your employee's spouse. Your company may sometimes permit executives to take their spouses along on business trips — you may think that doing so makes good business sense (and you may want to take your own spouse on business trips) — but for tax purposes, the cost of the spouse's trip is *never* a bona fide business expense (unless the spouse is also an employee with a business reason for going on the trip). If your company pays for a spouse's trip, that payment is not made under an accountable plan, and it is considered employee wages.

The most common travel expense problem under the business connection requirement, however, is the business trip that is partially a pleasure trip or that becomes a pleasure trip. Suppose that, as the president of your company, you must travel to Miami for business meetings on Thursday and Friday, and that you decide to go fishing in the Everglades over the weekend, as well. Your company reimburses you for the whole trip. You now have a tax problem. Since the purpose of the trip was primarily business, the airfare is a bona fide business expense, and the cost of food and lodging for Thursday and Friday, and possibly Saturday morning, is a bona fide business expense. But once you set out for the Everglades, the trip takes on a new character: Now it has become a pleasure trip, and nothing that you spend from this point on is a bona fide business expense. The expenses that your company reimburses once the trip becomes a pleasure trip are not made under an accountable plan and are wages to you.

It is here that the accounting aspects of the accountable plan rules become important. If your company reimburses both your business and your nonbusiness expenses but draws a distinction between them — for example, it reimburses you with two checks; or if it gives you only one check but provides a statement describing which portion of the reimbursement is for business and which portion is for nonbusiness expenses — then (assuming that you meet the other accountable plan requirements, discussed next) only the nonbusiness portion of the reimbursement is wages. However, if your company does not draw this distinction, *the entire reimbursement is considered wages*. Therefore, when you (or your other employees) submit a request for reimbursement of the money you spent on the trip, the expenses must be broken down between business and pleasure. Or if your spouse accompanied you on the trip, you must segregate her expenses from yours. If your accounting system cannot or does not make these distinctions, the entire reimbursement is considered a wage payment.

Establishing a Business Connection to Entertainment Expenses

Entertainment expenses are another category of business expense that might not be bona fide for tax purposes. It may be your company's policy to pay for your employee's theater or baseball tickets while he is in New York on business — it's good for the morale of employees working away from home. This is well and good from a business standpoint, but not from a tax standpoint. Entertainment expenses are not deductible as business expenses if your employee is merely entertaining himself. Any reimbursement of such expenses fails the business connection requirement and is not made under an accountable plan.

Some entertainment expenses are bona fide business expenses under the tax laws — and these are discussed shortly. If your company reimburses both deductible and nondeductible entertainment expenses, but distinguishes between the two using separate checks (or by providing a statement with the reimbursement) then only the reimbursement of the nondeductible expenses is considered wages. But if no such distinction is drawn, the entire reimbursement is considered a wage payment.

MISTAKE 22
▶ Disregarding the business connection rule when company credit cards are used.

Some businesspeople think that the business connection requirement applies only if they actually reimburse their employee's travel or entertainment expenses with a check, and that the accountable plan rules can be dispensed with if their employee charges his expenses on a company credit card. Not true. Charging an expense on a company credit card does not automatically make it a bona fide business expense. Even though you never actually reimburse an employee who charges an expense on the company credit card, that expense must still satisfy the business connection requirement and be accounted for under an accountable plan. The accountable plan rules ask whether company funds are being used for nonbusiness purposes; the method by which those funds are disbursed is not important.

MISTAKE 23
▶ Failing to substantiate the business or entertainment expense.

In order to be an accountable plan, your system of reimbursing employees for their business expenses must also require the *substantiation* of the expenses it reimburses. Again, for many expenses, common sense dictates the extent of this substantiation. An employee who asks for reimbursement of the money he spent to rent a television monitor for a sales presentation might be required to produce a receipt and a short note describing the purpose of the expenditure. That kind of substantiation will also satisfy the IRS. For travel and entertainment expenses, however, the IRS has specific substantiation requirements. These specific requirements also apply to expenses involving the use of automobiles, computers, or "entertainment facilities" (boats, country clubs); that is, they apply to all expenses that might represent you or your key employees enjoying themselves at the company's expense. Any such expenses not substantiated under these requirements constitute wages.

Substantiating Travel Expenses

In order to meet the substantiation requirement of the accountable plan rules for travel expenses, you must require your employees to substantiate four "elements" of their travel expenses:

1. The *amount* of each travel expenditure must be proven with documents. There must be a receipt (or some other document showing the amount of the expense) for all lodging expenses and for all other expenses in excess of $75; a document is required for each separate expenditure. As a practical matter, a receipt showing the amount of the expense is an absolute prerequisite to substantiating a travel expense. Without a receipt, you cannot, as far as the IRS is concerned, substantiate the amount of the expense

(unless you have statements from witnesses or other corroborating evidence—which you are not likely to have). If your employee says that he paid $100 for lodging but lost the receipt, he can't substantiate the amount of the expense. If you reimburse him for it, you make a wage payment subject to payroll taxes.

2. The *business purpose* of the travel must be established. Receipts prove only that an expenditure was made; they do not usually show why it was made. A bill from a hotel will show how much money you spent during two nights in a particular city, but were you there to see a ball game or to close a deal? You must be able to prove the business purpose of the travel. It is easy to remember why you took a trip soon after you took it, but the IRS will require you to remember the purpose of a trip three or four years later, when it is auditing your expense account. And then you probably won't remember. So the government suggests that you have a diary, a statement of expenses, trip sheets, or some other contemporaneous record that explains the purpose of the trip. A memorandum from the employee, stating what he did and who he saw (and why) while on the trip is usually the best way to prove this element of business travel.

A written document is not an absolute requirement for substantiating the business purpose of the trip (unlike a receipt, which is virtually an absolute requirement for documenting the amount of the expense). You can try years later to describe the business purpose in your own words, but contemporaneous written evidence is more probative of the purpose of the trip than oral evidence alone. As a practical matter, if you don't have written evidence, the IRS is less likely to believe your story, and you may fail to substantiate the business purpose of the travel.

3. The *period* of the travel must be documented. Airline ticket passenger receipts and hotel bills will usually provide this documentation, but if your employee drives his own car and stays with friends or relatives, you may have trouble, years later, recalling when, exactly, the business trip took place. Or if an employee's business trip turned into a pleasure trip, you must be able to establish the point in time when that occurred so that you can document the period of the business travel.

4. The *place* of the business travel must be documented. This requirement is easy if your employee goes to only one place at a time. But if he makes a circuit, sometimes flying, sometimes driving, it may be difficult to reconstruct the trip after several years without a memorandum in the file stating what happened.

Substantiating the business purpose of a trip is not a particularly burdensome task, but it can become one if you fail to stay on top of documentation. What is easy to do the day after a business trip becomes a real chore several weeks later, and it may not get done at all. If it doesn't get done, then the reimbursement of the expense is considered a wage payment.

Substantiating Entertainment Expenses

Entertainment expenses are substantiated with essentially the same four elements as travel expenses, modified slightly to account for the different nature of the expense, and there is a fifth and sometimes a sixth element peculiar to entertainment expenses. Your employees must show

1. the *amount* of each separate expenditure for the entertainment;
2. the *time* of the entertainment;
3. the *exact location* and the type of the entertainment; and
4. the *business reason* for the entertainment and (except for business meals when the employee is traveling on business and dining alone) the nature of any business discussion or activity.

Entertainment expenses are bona fide business expenses only when someone besides you or your employee is being entertained; thus, the fifth element that must be established in the case of entertainment expenses is the *business relationship* of the person entertained. (This element is also designed to prevent your employee from submitting an expense for lunch with his college roommate of twenty years ago.)

Therefore, if you went golfing with the owner of your most important client and wanted to deduct the cost of the green fees and the drinks afterward, you would have to show the amount paid for the green fees and the amount paid for the drinks separately; you would have to show the date and the place of the game; you would have to show the nature of the business you talked about; and you would have to provide information to establish the business connection, such as your guest's name, his position, and the relationship of his company to you. Otherwise, the reimbursement for the expense would not be made under an accountable plan.

A sixth element of an entertainment expense must be substantiated when the entertainment precedes or follows a business meeting. The cost of entertainment of a nature that is not conducive to business discussions — such as the theater or a ball game — is still deductible if the entertainment occurs immediately before or after a business meeting. When it does, however, you must document not only the entertainment, in the manner just described, but you must also document the time, place, and business purpose of the business meeting that immediately preceded or followed it.

Substantiating Car and Computer Expenses

Separate substantiation rules apply when you reimburse your employees for the cost of using their own property in your business. This property is called *listed property* because it is on an IRS list of property that is susceptible to both business and personal use. Listed property includes cars (or other modes of transportation), computers and cellular phones, and property that is typically used for entertainment or recreation, such as a boat.

Suppose your employee drives his own car while working for you, uses his own cellular telephone, or works at home at night on his own computer. You may choose to reimburse some of his expenses associated with these properties: You might pay him 30 cents per mile for the business use of his car or so many dollars per month toward the cost of a computer or a cellular phone. If you don't want these reimbursements to be treated as wages, and if your employee wants to claim an above-the-line deduction for his costs for the property, then the business use and cost of the property must be substantiated just as travel and entertainment expenses are — under an accountable plan.

Here, too, to qualify for reimbursements for the use of listed property four elements must be substantiated:

1. The amount of each separate expenditure with respect to the property, such as the cost of acquisition or lease payments or the cost of maintenance and repairs.
2. The extent of the business use of the property — mileage for cars, for example, or hours or days for computers.
3. Time: the date of the expenditure or of the business use.
4. The business purpose of the expenditure or the usage.

It's not enough for your employee to say he drove his car 50 miles or used his computer 10 hours per week on business. It's not enough for you to tell an IRS agent that an employee "works at home a lot on his computer so we pay him extra money to cover the cost of the computer." Details of the use must be provided: You must be able to tell the IRS where he went and whom he saw in his car; and what kind of work he did on his computer, and when he did it.

These are the substantiation requirements of the accountable plan rules. If you do not meet these requirements, you do not have an accountable plan, and the reimbursements you have made to your employees are wages. If these substantiation requirements are met for some expenses but not for others, then the reimbursement must distinguish between expenses that have been substantiated and those that have not, and the latter reimbursements are considered wages. If this distinction is not made, the entire reimbursement is considered a wage payment subject to payroll taxes.

MISTAKE 24
▶ **Failing to make your employees return unsubstantiated business expense advances.**

Finally, if your company advances money for traveling or other business expenses to your employees before they actually incur the expenses, or reimburses them before they substantiate the expense, then to have an accountable plan, you must require that your employees return the money for any expense that they cannot substantiate (the return requirement). If you don't require that unsubstantiated advances be returned, then *all* of the advances are considered wages.

Not only must business expenses be returned if they are not substantiated; they must also be either substantiated or returned "within a reasonable period of time." If the expenses are not substantiated within a reasonable period of time (and not returned), then they are treated as wages. A reasonable period of time depends on (you guessed it) the facts and circumstances; that is, on the amount of the travel or other expenses in question, the organization of your company, and the number of employees that you must deal with. The more complex your organization, the longer the return time that is still considered reasonable. However, there are two safe-harbor rules. If you meet either one of them, you pass the reasonable time rule of the return requirement:

1. If your company advances funds within 30 days of when the expense is actually incurred, and requires either that substantiation be provided within 60 days after the expense is incurred, or that the unsubstantiated funds be returned within 120 days after the expense is incurred, you meet the first safe-harbor test.
2. If your company provides its employees with periodic (at least quarterly) statements of their travel or other business expense accounts and requires them to substantiate or return any unsubstantiated expenses within 120 days after the statement is provided, you meet the second safe-harbor test.

You never meet the return requirement if you advance funds that do not approximate the amount of expenses to be incurred, or if you advance funds unreasonably far in advance of the time that the expenses are expected to be incurred. In effect, if you provide your employees with funds "on the float," you fail the return requirement, and the entire advance constitutes wages. What is more likely to occur is that you simply pay yourself $2,000 on the first day of each month to cover travel and entertainment expenses for the month, in which case the entire payment is considered a wage.

Having the appropriate return requirements in place is, of course, only part of the solution. You also have to get back the unsubstantiated expenses. And, years later, during an IRS audit, many employers learn that they never did recover those unsubstantiated expenses, and then they have to pay payroll taxes on the expenses at that time.

MISTAKE 25
▶ **Overpaying per diem reimbursements.**

Many people find the first element of the travel expense substantiation rules — the requirement that the amount of the expense be proven — to be very burdensome. It's too much trouble to document every dollar spent on food and gasoline and to keep sheaves of paperwork on hotel and other travel costs. For people who think this way, there is an alternative system for documenting travel expenses: the *per diem rule*. If your company uses the per diem rule, then you don't have to document the amount of the travel expense, and you don't have to keep all those receipts.

Under the per diem rule, your company simply pays your employee an IRS-approved per diem for each day of business travel — and then you're done. The amount of the travel expenses need not be substantiated. Your employee is paid a flat sum for each day of business travel to cover his lodging, meals, and incidental expenses such as laundry or telephone calls (transportation expenses are still documented separately), and that sum is deemed to be substantiated without any actual documentation of the amount he spends. If he spends less than the per diem amount, he gets to keep the excess, tax-free; if he spends more than the per diem amount, too bad — he cannot deduct any additional expenses even if he can prove that he made them. But under the per diem rule, he needn't come home with packages of receipts. The amount of the travel expense is one figure — the per diem that you pay him.

The maximum amount of the per diem allowance that can be paid under the per diem system is the allowance paid by the federal government to its own employees. The government publishes these per diem rates each year (your tax adviser can get them for you), and they vary from one locality to another. They're generally higher in metropolitan areas and resort areas and lower in other areas.

Businesspeople who use the per diem rule get into trouble because they overpay per diem rates. If your company pays a rate that exceeds the government's per diem rate, only the amount of the government rate is deemed substantiated. Any amount in excess of the government rate will be treated as wages; you are required to pay and withhold payroll taxes on per diem reimbursements over the government rate. And your employee will have to report the excess as income. (He can then claim, as itemized deductions, any expenses that he can substantiate.)

If you pay your employees less than the government per diem rate, only the amount actually paid is deem substantiated. If your employee spends more than that, he can claim an itemized deduction for the excess expenses as long as he can substantiate them.

MISTAKE 26
◗ Paying per diem rates to yourself.

Owners of businesses are not permitted to reimburse their own travel expenses under the per diem rules. They are required to produce receipts for each expenditure for which they are reimbursed. All per diems paid to business owners are wages unless the owners have receipts to cover the per diem allowance. An owner of a business, for purposes of this rule, is anyone who owns more than 10 percent of the business.

MISTAKE 27
◗ Overlooking the other substantiation rules when you use per diem reimbursements.

Another common mistake made by business owners who use the per diem rules is that they forget that the per diem rates eliminate only the need to substantiate the amount of the expense and that all the other accountable plan rules continue to apply. When the per diem rules are used, the business purpose of the trip must still be substantiated, the time and the place of the trip must still be shown, and the return requirement still applies. If your employee fails to substantiate the purpose and time and place of the expenditure and does not return any unsubstantiated per diem amounts that he has received, then the entire per diem allowance is a wage payment to him, subject to payroll taxes and includible in his income.

None of the rules changes when per diems are used, except that receipts are no longer necessary. As with dollar-for-dollar reimbursements of employee business expenses, your employees may be able to meet the substantiation requirements for some, but not all, of their per diem allowances. The portion of the allowance that can be substantiated will be tax-free; the unsubstantiated portion will be taxable, unless it is returned in a reasonable time. Therefore, if your employee traveled on Thursday, Friday, and Saturday but could not establish a business purpose for the Saturday travel, the per diem allowance for Thursday and Friday would still be tax-free. But if he didn't return the Saturday allowance, then that allowance would be considered wages.

MISTAKE 28
♦ Not having a written accountable plan.

When the IRS comes in to audit your business and you have claimed substantial deductions for travel and entertainment expenses, you can be absolutely sure that those expenses will be audited. The agent will ask you: "Have you got an accountable plan?" If you say, "Huh?" you're in trouble. If he asks a traveling employee: "What's the system for returning travel advances that you can't document?" and the employee says: "What are you talking about?" you're in big trouble. So if you don't have a system for accounting for travel expenses, get one. You can put it in your employee manual, you can post it on the bulletin board, you can send a periodic memo to those employees who travel. Your plan doesn't have to be a leather-bound book or a part of an employment contract. It doesn't even have to be written down; but if, when the agent asks if you have a plan, you hand him a copy of it, you're one step ahead in the audit. If he sees that you have enough sense to have a written plan, he may decide that it's not worth his time to audit the travel expenses in the first place.

Chapter Six

Cars, Planes, and Other Fringe Benefits

For many people, fringe benefits, or perquisites, are a major reason for owning a business or for working for someone who does. At one time "perks" were such an integral part of the American business experience that when the IRS proposed in the 1970s to require people to pay tax on their fringe benefits, Congress promptly passed a law prohibiting it from doing so. The idea of taxing perks was simply too hot a political potato to be left to the bureaucrats. Ten years and another trillion dollars in national debt later, Congress changed its tune and enacted legislation that taxed most perks, and this law is still in effect today.

If a perk is taxable, it is treated as a wage payment. It is subject to social security taxes and income tax withholding. If you provide a taxable perk but do not pay and collect payroll taxes on it, your business will owe the IRS a lot of money if your fringe benefit program is examined in an audit. And as with other failures to keep up with payroll taxes, you may end up paying your employees' taxes.

MISTAKE 29
◗ Not understanding whether a perk is tax-free.

Some perks may be tax-free, depending on the circumstances under which they are provided, but only a small number of employer-provided fringe benefits are *always* tax free. The always tax-free perks include the following:

- Medical and disability insurance premiums that you pay on behalf of your employees to provide them with insurance coverage.
- Premiums that you pay for group-term life insurance for up to $50,000 in coverage.
- Lodging and meals that you provide to employees who are required as a part of their job to live or dine on your business premises.
- On-premises athletic facilities that are used by your employees or their families.

The value of these benefits is excluded from your employees' income, and is not considered a wage payment by your company.

All other benefits of value that you provide to your employees are potentially taxable to them as wages; and if you provide any perks other than those on the preceding list, you must determine whether they are taxable. The use of a company car, discounts on company products or services, tickets to entertainment or sporting events, a weekend at the company's fishing lodge, country club memberships, and others are potentially taxable. I say potentially because under designated conditions, many of these benefits are not taxable to your employees. Meeting those designated conditions is the hard part, and I turn to that now.

MISTAKE 30
▶ **Paying too many small perks.**

Perks with such a small value that accounting for them simply isn't worth the trouble—so called *de minimus* fringe benefits—are tax-free. Congress had the Christmas turkey in mind when it enacted this exclusion. Once it passed a law that taxed all perks, it had to avoid being ridiculous. Free coffee in the office would also fall within the de minimus rule, as would the company picnic or an occasional office party. But in determining whether a perk has de minimus value, you must take into account the frequency with which it is provided. If you give your employees a free turkey every Friday, the total value might not be so small. There is no harm in giving an employee your tickets to a ball game that you cannot attend; season tickets would be another matter.

A low-cost cafeteria where your employees can have lunch is a special category of a de minimus fringe benefit. The benefit of inexpensive lunches in the company cafeteria is not a taxable perk as long as the cafeteria is not operated at a loss. The revenues your company derives from the cafeteria must at least equal the cost of operating it. If your cafeteria does lose money, then the savings that your employees enjoy there are taxable as wages. Also, for low-cost lunches to be tax-free perks to your employees, they must not be restricted to highly compensated employees. The executive dining room is no longer a tax-free perk.

MISTAKE 31
▶ **Giving employees too large a discount.**

The value of a discount that you offer to employees on company products—so-called qualified employee discounts—is not a taxable perk, as long as the discount is within permitted limits. The official description of the permitted limits is as follows: The percentage discount that you offer your employees cannot exceed the sale price of the product to customers, less its cost to you, divided by the sale price to customers. This essentially means that you cannot sell products to your employees at a price that is below your cost. (For example, if you sell a product to customers for $60 and you pay $40 for it, the employee discount cannot exceed one-third ($60 − $40/$60.) If the discount exceeds the permitted limit, the excess amount of the discount is considered a taxable perk.

Company services can also be provided to employees at a discount, tax-free, as long as the discount is not more than 20 percent. If the discount exceeds 20 percent, the excess amount of the discount allowed is considered a taxable wage. Also, to avoid tax on products and services offered at a discount, the discounts must be available to employees other than just highly compensated employees (as in the case of the low-cost company cafeteria).

MISTAKE 32
❯ Failing to define the working condition fringe benefit.

Working condition fringe benefits are tax-free. This exception to the general rule that perks are taxable is the most important exception. It is the one that gives you the tax-free use of company-provided cars, boats, planes, theater tickets, and other perks, which you figure, as the owner of the business, you ought to be entitled to anyway.

A working condition fringe benefit is any property or service provided to an employee that, if the employee had paid for it himself, would have been deductible as a business expense or would have been a depreciable cost. For example, if your employee uses his own car in your business, the cost of the car allocable to business use is a deductible expense to him: He can deduct the operating costs of the car that are allocable to business use, he can depreciate the business-use portion of the cost of the car, or he can claim a cents-per-mile deduction for business mileage.

If, instead, you provide your employee (including yourself if you run your business through a corporation) with a car, the value of the use of the car for business is a tax-free working condition fringe benefit. Another example: If your employee bought a computer so that he could work at home in the evenings, he could depreciate the portion of the cost of the computer allocable to business use (as long as he used it more than half the time for business purposes). If you give him a computer, the value of the use of the computer for business is a tax-free working condition fringe benefit.

But now comes the catch that many business owners overlook: The value of the use of the car or the computer is tax-free only to the extent that your employee uses it for business. If he uses the car only half the time for business (and half the time for personal purposes), then only half the value of the car is a tax-free working condition fringe benefit, and the other half is *taxable compensation*. If you drive a car owned by your company and use it 50 percent of the time for business and 50 percent of the time for personal matters, you have income equal to half the value of the car, and your company has made a wage payment, subject to payroll taxes, equal to half the value of the car.

How do you keep track of which portion of the value of the car is a tax-free working condition fringe benefit? You might have guessed: There are "substantiation" rules.

MISTAKE 33
◗ **Failing to substantiate the working condition that makes the perk tax-free.**

The substantiation rules for the working condition fringe benefit are similar to those for travel and entertainment expenses covered in Chapter 5. It is not necessary, however, to have the accountable plan described in Chapter 5 because, in the case of a perk, there is no expenditure to document and, obviously, there is no return requirement for undocumented expenditures. But the other elements of business use must be documented: the time and place of the business use and the business purpose of the perk. To the extent business usage is not substantiated, the value of the perk is considered wages. So if you send a computer home with an employee, he had better keep a log of when and why he uses it for business and to what extent, if any, he uses it to balance his checkbook or play computer games, because some day the IRS may ask for such substantiation. The burden of proof is on you, the owner. If you provide your employee with a working condition fringe benefit, the value of the benefit is considered a wage payment except to the extent you can document business use.

MISTAKE 34
◗ **Failing to determine whether you should be providing a perk.**

Because perks not excluded from income generate both income tax and employment tax liability, employers who have the opportunity to provide perks must ask themselves whether it makes any sense to do so. It might be better for everyone to just charge the employee the market value of the perk and then return the money as a bonus. That way everybody knows what the score is; the value is established, and no back taxes become due. One employer had a ski house in Vermont that he frequently let clients use. When clients weren't using it, he and his top executives and their families used it — weekends and holidays, winter and summer. Over a three-year period, his employees racked up 100 days of winter use at a value of $300 per day and 170 other days at a value of $150 per day. This totalled $55,500 in compensation, fully subject to income tax withholding (at about 20 percent) and to the 2.9 percent social security tax (all employees earned a salary above the wage base). With interest and penalties, the tax bill came to just under $25,000. Had he charged his employees for the use of the ski house, then returned the money as bonuses, his cost would have been only $800 (1.45 percent of $55,000). For the employees, this arrangement would have ended up costing about $90 per day for winter use (assuming they paid an average tax of about 30 percent on the $300 bonus) or $45 per day for summer use (about 30 percent of $150). Ninety dollars per day for a ski house in Vermont is still a good deal for the employee — certainly a better deal than the bill the employer got from the IRS. (Note that, instead of collecting the rent and returning it, the employer could simply credit the employee with income equal to the value of the use of the house, but then the employer must come up with the cash to withhold the income and employee-paid social security taxes.)

MISTAKE 35
▶ **Misvaluing the perk.**

If a fringe benefit is not excluded from income, then a value has to be placed on it. In the case of reimbursed business expenses, determining a value is not a problem because the value is fixed by the amount of the reimbursement. If you reimburse your employee

$200 for car expenses during the year, and he fails to document his expenditures or to substantiate the business purpose, the amount of additional compensation is clear: It is $200. But suppose, instead, you provide him with a car for the year. If he establishes the business use of the car, it is a working condition fringe benefit and (at least for tax purposes) you don't care what it's worth. To the extent that he can't prove business use, it is a taxable fringe benefit, and then you must know what it is worth.

The general valuation rule for a perk — the dollar amount that an employee must include in income (and that you must treat as wages) if the perk is not for some reason excluded from income — is its fair market value. In other words, what it would cost your employee if he went out and acquired it himself. That's the general rule, and it is the rule used for most perks. But there are special rules for automobiles. In the case of automobiles, you have a choice of valuation methods, and choosing the wrong one can be costly.

The general valuation rule *can* be used for automobiles, and if you do use it, you would determine what it would cost in your area to lease the vehicle for a year (assuming the employee has the use of the car for a full year), and multiply that cost by the percentage of personal use. The result would be the value of the fringe benefit.

If you don't want to figure out what the car could be leased for in your area, you can use the IRS's special *automobile lease valuation* rule. Under this special rule, the value of the use of the car is its *Annual Lease Value* as determined under a table provided by the

IRS. To use this table, you first figure out the car's fair market value at the time you turn it over to your employee. Then you derive its Annual Lease Value by reading the IRS table. For example, an automobile with a fair market value of between $12,000 and $12,999 has, according to the IRS table, an Annual Lease Value of $3,600. That is the value of the use of the car. If your employee uses it 20 percent for personal reasons, the amount of the taxable fringe benefit is $720 (20 percent of $3,600). A car with a fair market value of between $20,000 to $20,999 has an Annual Lease Value of $5,600. These figures are all right there in the IRS table, and it is an alluringly simple way of figuring out the value of the use of a car.

But there is a hidden cost in the IRS tables. The IRS's Annual Lease Value method of valuing an automobile perk assumes that the employer is not only providing the car but also paying for the maintenance and insurance for the car, so the value obtained for the car under the Annual Lease Value method is higher than the value you would get if you used the general valuation method. Even if the employee pays for maintenance and insurance, you cannot reduce the Annual Lease Value to reflect that he pays these costs. Therefore, if the employee does pay for maintenance and insurance, it is to your advantage to forgo the Annual Lease Value method and value the car under the general rules of valuation, which do not include maintenance and insurance. By doing so, you are viewed as paying your employee a smaller amount of wages, thus you pay less social security tax.

MISTAKE 36
♦ Using the cents-per-mile rule when it's not permitted.

Another way to value the use of a car for personal purposes is the *cents-per-mile* valuation method. Under this method, you multiply the number of miles of personal use by the IRS-published standard mileage rate for the year (that rate is about 31 cents and is subject to change each year); the product is the value of the fringe benefit. This method is so simple that you might wonder why everybody doesn't use it. The answer is that not everybody is permitted to use it. The Annual Lease Value method can always be used, but the cents-per-mile method can be used only if one of the following conditions is met:

1. The employer expects that the car will be used regularly in his business throughout the year (or throughout the portion of the year that he owns or leases it).
2. The car is driven at least 10,000 miles during the year (proportionately fewer miles if the car is owned or leased for only a portion of the year), is used primarily by employees (not primarily by their spouses or children), and is not an "expensive" car. Use of the car by the employee for commuting to work counts toward the 10,000-mile requirement (although the value of commuting use is a taxable perk). An "expensive" car is one that costs more than about $14,000 (this figure is adjusted each year for inflation).

This cents-per-mile rule, then, is limited to situations in which personal use is expected to be minimal (condition 1) or to situations in which, though personal use may not be minimal, overall the car is expected to be driven a large number of business miles (condition 2). If you have used the cents-per-mile rule but have not met one of the conditions for doing so, you will have to recompute the value of the perk under another method. Or if the car is an "expensive" car, you will have to recalculate the value of the perk under the Annual Lease Value method or the general method of valuation—and because the car has a high value, you are likely to get a larger figure for the value of the perk and consequently likely to owe more in payroll tax.

Like the Annual Lease Value method, the cents-per-mile method of valuation assumes that the employer is paying for maintenance and insurance, and the value obtained under the cents-per-mile method cannot be reduced to reflect any contribution by the employee to those costs. The cents-per-mile method assumes that the employer is paying for gasoline, as well, but if the employee buys his own gas, the cents-per-mile rate may be reduced by 5.5 cents.

Chapter Seven

Home-Office Deductions

When you own a business, you assume that you have a nearly inalienable right to claim a deduction for the cost of keeping an office in your home. After all, you do a good deal of work there, important work that is best done in the quiet of your den away from the pressures of your office. Naturally, you think, you ought to get a tax break for that. The fact is, however, that a home-office deduction is available to business owners only under very limited circumstances. And when it comes to the home-office deduction, business owners get into trouble in two areas:

1. They fail to take the steps necessary to qualify for the deduction.
2. Even if they qualify for the deduction, they neglect to arrange their affairs so that the deduction is worth something to them.

IDENTIFYING EXCEPTIONS

MISTAKE 37
▶ **Failing to qualify for the home-office deduction.**

The general rule on the allowability of the home-office deduction is: *No deduction* is allowed for the cost of maintaining an office in your home. But there are three exceptions to the general rule. In order to claim a deduction for a home office, you must fall within one of these exceptions; otherwise no deduction is allowed.

The Principal Place of Business Exception

If you use a portion of your home as the principal place of your business, you will be allowed to take the home-office deduction. Common sense tells you that this exception will not ordinarily apply to people with an office in a location away from their home. That location will normally be the principal place of their business. The principal place of business exception applies to very small businesses with no other business location — an author, a consultant, or an accountant, who works out of his home and has no other regular place of business.

For people who regularly work in more than one location, the principal place of their business is determined under current law by considering two factors: where they do the most important aspect of their work (the "essence" of their work); and how much time they spend in each location. If the essence of your work is performed at home and you spend most of your time there, your home office will be your principal place of business. But Congress has changed the definition of "principal place of business" for years starting after 1998: after 1998 the principal place of your business will be the place where you perform the administrative or management activities of your business (assuming that there is no other fixed location where such activities are performed to any substantial extent).

The Client Meeting Exception

If you use an office in your home to meet with clients or customers (or, in the case of doctors, with patients), the home-office deduction will also be available to you. Your home office need not be the principal place of your business; you may have your main office somewhere else, as long as you use your home office to meet with clients or customers. Occasional meetings, however, are not sufficient to make this exception apply; your use of your home office for meetings must be a substantial and integral part of the way you conduct your business. Note this important point of contention: The IRS says that your customers must be physically present at these meetings in order for this exception to apply—that meetings over the telephone from your home office don't count. However, the courts say that telephone meetings do count. In either event, if you intend to rely on this exception, be prepared to substantiate the use of your home office for client meetings with a log book that shows when those meetings occurred, who was present, and why.

The Separate Structure Exception

If you work at home in an office that is not attached to your home (it must be a free-standing structure), the home-office deduction will be available. This exception will be the one most likely to apply to people who own their own businesses. A separate structure doesn't have to be your principal place of business, and you don't have to meet clients or customers there. The only requirement for the separate structure exception is that you use the separate structure in connection with your business—that is, you work there.

Congress provided the separate structure exception because it reasoned that if you went to the trouble and incurred the cost of building a separate structure, chances are you really needed the place for your business. Of course, anyone who owned a poolhouse at the time that Congress enacted the home-office rule immediately outfitted the place with a desk and a typewriter, and had a home office subject to the separate structure exception.

If you are not self-employed—if you work for a corporation, even your own corporation—then falling under one of these three exceptions to the general rule is still not enough. As an employee, you have a special hurdle to clear: The use of an office in your home must be "for the convenience of your employer."

MISTAKE 38
▶ **Failing the convenience of the employer test.**

People who are employed by someone else — including yourself if you work for your corporation — can claim a home-office deduction only if they work at home "for the convenience of" their employer.

The convenience of the employer test is met if any one of the following conditions exists:

1. Having a home office is required as a condition of employment.
2. Having a home office is necessary for the proper functioning of the business.
3. Having a home office is necessary to allow the employee to properly perform his duties.

When you are the owner of the business that employs you, you will probably have to meet the second or third condition; after all, requiring yourself to have a home office (the first condition) will seem self-serving unless there is an objective, compelling reason for doing so. Business owners have met the third condition, however, by arguing that, to properly perform such duties as long-term planning and strategic thinking, they needed a quiet place away from the main office.

On the assumption that as a business owner you

often work nights and weekends, it might also be "necessary" to have a home office (the second condition) if your main office isn't usable after regular hours because the heat or air conditioning is turned off, or there is inadequate security, or because your main office is too far from your home to return to after dinner with your family.

The convenience of the employer test can therefore sometimes be met by business owners, but, like reasonable compensation questions, some thought has to be given to how you meet it.

MISTAKE 39
▶ Failing to use your home office regularly and exclusively for business.

Assuming that you fall within one of the exceptions (and, if you are an employee, meet the convenience test), you then have another hurdle to clear. The portion of your home that constitutes your principal place of business, or where you meet with clients, or that is a separate structure that you use for business purposes, must be devoted *exclusively* to your business and must be used for business purposes *regularly*.

The exclusivity rule eliminates your kitchen and bedroom as a home office. It eliminates your den if your children watch television there or if you watch television there for your own enjoyment. A room, or a divisible part of a room, passes the exclusivity test only if it is used for no purpose other than your business. A spare bedroom that you have converted to an office (and that, literally, is never used by guests), a study that is off limits to other family members, or a refurbished basement area that only you may enter are the kinds of places in your home that may qualify as home offices, provided that you do not use the place yourself for purposes other than business.

Using your home office occasionally for business purposes will not entitle you to a home-office deduction either, because of the requirement that the office be used regularly for business purposes. Not only must you use your home office exclusively for business, but you must use it regularly, as well. Regular use does not mean that it must be used every day, only that it must be used, well, regularly. Two or three times per week would probably suffice, or even two weeks out of every month. A pattern of use is what is required—and documentation establishing the pattern.

MISTAKE 40
◆ Failing to make the value of the home-office deduction worthwhile.

Being entitled to a home-office deduction because you fall within one of the exceptions is only half the battle. The other half is making the deduction worth something.

What is deductible? All of the expenses of maintaining a home office are potentially deductible. (Whether they can in fact be deducted is discussed next.) The beauty of the home-office deduction is that most deductible home-office expenses are those that you would incur anyway and that would not normally be deductible but that suddenly become deductible because you have an office in your home.

Deductible home-office expenses fall into two categories: expenses relating to your entire home, a portion of which are allocable to your home office, and expenses relating solely to your home office.

Your heating and cooling bills are examples of usually nondeductible expenses that relate to your entire home. These bills are deductible to the extent that they are allocable to your home office. If your office occupies one room of an eight-room home, one-eighth of your heating and cooling bill would be a deductible home-office expense. (You can also allocate such expenses based on the square footage of your home office.) One-eighth of your homeowner's insurance premiums would also be deductible, as would one-eighth of your housecleaning costs. One-eighth of your mortgage interest payments and real estate taxes would also be deductible as home-office expenses (though these expenses can also be claimed as itemized deductions). And you could depreciate one-eighth of your tax basis in your home.

Expenses allocable to a particular portion of your home other than your home office, such as the repair of a broken window in the kitchen, would not qualify as home-office deductions. Expenses related solely to your home office would be fully deductible. The cost of fixing a broken window in your office or of painting just your office would be fully deductible.

What is actually deducted? *Potentially* deductible home-office expenses are exactly that: potentially deductible. There are two limitations on the amount of home-office expenses that can actually be claimed. The first limitation is based on the amount of income that you earn: Home-office deductions cannot exceed the amount of income earned while you are in your home office. If you have another principal office, you must determine the portion of your salary or income that is earned at your home office, and this amount sets the ceiling on your home-office deductions. For example, if you meet clients in your home office or work at home in a separate structure, and you figure that 10 percent of your total income of $100,000, or $10,000, results from work done at your home office, then no more than $10,000 in home-office deductions can actually be deducted. Before counting your tax savings from the home-office deduction, therefore, you must give some thought to how much of your income you can justifiably allocate to your home office and how you will justify it. Home-office deductions can be claimed only against income that is allocable to the home office. If you cannot justify the allocation of enough income to your home office to cover the deductions you would like to claim, the IRS will disallow home-office deductions without even looking at the nature of the deductions.

Where your home office is your principal place of business, the ceiling on home-office deductions is the net income from your business, disregarding home-office expenses. So if your home office is the principal place of a business that has a net income of $20,000 for the year (gross income less business expenses other than the home-office expenses), your home-office deductions cannot exceed $20,000.

The rule that home-office deductions cannot exceed

the amount of net income earned at (or attributable to) your home office simply means that you cannot create a loss from your home-office activities and use that loss to reduce tax on income from other activities. However, if in any year the amount of your home-office deductions does exceed the income attributable to your home office, you can carry the excess forward to the next year and, subject to the same limitations, claim those excess deductions against home-office income in the next year. And you can keep carrying unused home-office deductions forward until you are able to use them.

The second limitation on deducting home-office expenses is that expenses such as insurance premiums or heating bills or depreciation, which may be claimed only because of your home office, must be claimed *after* you have claimed expenses that are always deductible even if you don't have a home office. These so-called always deductible expenses usually consist of home mortgage interest and real estate taxes. To return to the example of your eight-room house: If your mortgage interest and real estate tax payments came to $16,000 for the year, you would have to reduce your net income attributable to your home office by $2,000 ($16,000/8) before you could claim any other home-office expenses. If the net income from your business was $20,000, your deductible home-office expenses, apart from the always-deductible expenses, could not exceed $18,000. To summarize: Your total home-office expenses can't exceed your net income, and you must claim the always-deductible home-office expenses against that net income first.

Limitations on the amount of actually deductible home-office expenses will sometimes make a home office barely worth the trouble. If you allocate 10 percent of your $100,000 salary to your home office (that is, $10,000), and have $30,000 per year in mortgage interest and real estate taxes, of which $3,750 (one-eighth) is allocated to your home office, your deductible home-office expenses are limited to $6,350. Nothing to scoff at, but if you had larger savings in mind, you will be disappointed, and helpless to do anything about it. When you set up a home office, therefore, plan to use it enough to allocate sufficient income to it to make the home-office deduction worthwhile. And before you go to a lot of trouble to secure home-office deductions be sure that the always-deductible expenses won't consume all of that income and render the home-office deductions useless anyway.

Chapter Eight

Deducting Interest on Business Loans

Not all interest is deductible. *Personal interest*, interest paid on money borrowed to buy personal items such as clothing, gifts, artwork, furniture, and cars not used for business, is not deductible at all.

Investment interest, interest paid on money borrowed to make investments, is deductible only to the extent of investment income (income or gain from property held for investment). Therefore, if during the year, you paid $6,000 in investment interest but earned only $3,000 in investment income, only $3,000 of the interest is deductible (the remaining $3,000 in interest may be carried forward to future years and deducted against investment income earned in those future years). Investment interest is also a "miscellaneous itemized deduction," and, therefore, even if deductible, it can be claimed only to the extent that (together with any other miscellaneous itemized deductions) it exceeds 2 percent of your adjusted gross income.

Business interest, interest paid on money borrowed to use in a trade or business, is always deductible in full.

For the small-business owner, the goal is to separate business borrowings from investment or personal borrowings and, whenever possible, to borrow for or through the business. It is the failure to make this separation that gets businesspeople into trouble.

MISTAKE 41
▶ **Borrowing money yourself when your corporation needs money.**

People who run their businesses through corporations often make the mistake of taking out a loan themselves to obtain money that is needed by their corporations. If their business needs money, they borrow the money as individuals and put it into the corporation, either because the bank won't lend to the corporation or because they never think to have the corporation take out the loan in the first place.

Financing your business in this manner is likely to cost you interest deductions. For your corporation, the loan would be a business loan and the interest would be fully deductible. But not for you; for you, the stock you own in your own corporation is an investment for tax purposes, so when you borrow money and then put it into your corporation (either as a loan to the company or as a contribution to its capital), the loan is considered an *investment* loan, not a business loan, and the interest that you pay on the loan is considered investment interest, not business interest. It is deductible only to the extent that you earn investment income. This is fine if you have investment income, but if you don't, then you have lost an interest deduction that could have been claimed very easily by the corporation. Unless there are other compelling reasons, therefore, never borrow money yourself to obtain funds needed by your corporation. You should always let the corporation borrow the money, even if you have to guarantee the loan. (Different rules apply to S corporations, as we shall see toward the end of this chapter.)

MISTAKE 42
▶ **Borrowing money yourself to make investments when you own a corporation.**

Limitations on deducting investment interest don't apply to corporations. Those limitations apply only to individuals. If a corporation borrows money to invest in the stock market, therefore, all of the interest that it pays on the loan is deductible even if the corporation has no (or insufficient) investment income during the year. Consequently, if you run your business through a corporation (other than an S corporation) and you intend to borrow money to make an investment, consider doing so through your corporation so that the interest paid on the loan will be fully deductible. I say "consider" doing so because there are other factors to take into account as well. If the investment proves to be a good one, the profits end up in the corporation and may be subject to double taxation, once at the corporate level and again when they are distributed as a dividend. On the other hand, if you can pay those profits out to yourself as a salary, or if the corporation has losses that can offset the profits, double taxation may not occur, and it will have been worthwhile to secure the interest deduction for the corporation.

MISTAKE 43
◗ **Letting your corporation borrow money when you should have borrowed it yourself.**

Corporations by definition do not borrow money to acquire personal items. If a corporation buys a piece of furniture, the furniture is presumably for the company's office; and if the corporation borrows money to buy the furniture, the interest that it pays on the loan is still business interest. If the corporation gives the furniture to you to use in your home, that may be compensation to you, but it is still a business expense to the corporation, and the interest that it incurred to borrow the money to make the expenditure is still business interest. So why not have your corporation borrow money whenever you intend to buy something? Maybe you should, maybe not; it all depends on the arithmetic, and the mistake to avoid is forgetting to do the arithmetic.

Suppose you want to buy a car for your children — clearly a personal expenditure. If you borrow $15,000 to buy the car, at 8 percent interest, you have almost $1,200 in nondeductible interest expenses in the first year (smaller amounts of interest expense in later years as the loan is repaid). If the corporation borrows the money, all these interest deductions can be claimed by it. However, since it is you who needs the money to buy the car, your corporation has to get the money to you, presumably by paying you additional compensation of $15,000. That $15,000 in additional compensation will be considered part of your income, and it will generate additional income taxes of about $4,500. But since that compensation is also deductible by the corporation, the corporation should save about $4,500 in taxes. Assuming the corporation is able to use the deduction, it may make sense to have the corporation borrow the money and pay it to you. You pay tax on the compensation, but the corporation saves an offsetting amount of tax by deducting the compensation payment. And the corporation saves additional tax by deducting the interest on the loan, which you could not have done.

There's more, however. It would not make sense for the corporation to borrow the money if that additional $15,000 in compensation paid to you was subject to a 15.3 percent social security tax (discussed in Chapter 2). In this case, the government has simply ended up with another $3,000 of your money—an amount that is probably more than what the corporation will save in taxes over the years as it deducts the interest expenses—and nothing has been accomplished. So borrowing money through your corporation for personal reasons makes sense only if your salary exceeds the social security wage base so that the 15.3 percent payroll tax won't apply. The 2.9 percent payroll tax on wages in excess of the wage base will still apply but, depending on the arithmetic, it may be worthwhile to pay that tax.

THE TRACING RULES
(SOLE PROPRIETORSHIPS)

MISTAKE 44
▶ Failing to separate your business and investment borrowings.

When you run your businesses as a sole proprietorship and borrow money, the loan could be for business purposes or for investment or for personal purposes. After all, in a sole proprietorship, it is you, a human being, borrowing the money. You may borrow in the name of your company, but that is still just you signing for the loan. With sole proprietorships, therefore, it doesn't matter who borrows the money; what matters is what the money is used for. If it's used for your business, it's deductible; if it's used to make investments, it's deductible only against investment income; if it's used for personal purposes, it's not deductible at all.

People who run their businesses through sole proprietorships, therefore, must keep track of how they spend money that they borrow. Often they find they have lost deductions for interest that they thought was paid on a business loan because they did not keep track of how the loan proceeds were spent. They may have kept track from a common-sense standpoint, but not from a tax standpoint which, as we have seen by now, may have very little to do with common sense.

Sole proprietors may end up spending borrowed money for personal reasons — at least as far as the IRS is concerned — without even realizing it. Let's start with a simple example that does make sense. Suppose you borrow $20,000 and deposit it into your business's bank account (assuming for the time being that when you make the deposit you have no other funds in the account), then write a check for $5,000 to pay for your children's tuition, and spend the remaining $15,000 on supplies and inventory for your business. It is fairly plain to see that only the interest on $15,000 of the loan is deductible as business interest. The interest on the remaining $5,000 is personal interest — because the funds were spent for personal purposes — and so is not deductible at all.

Now suppose that you just had a slight cash flow problem when you spent that $5,000 on tuition, and a few days later a customer pays you $5,000, which you deposit into the same account and spend on your business. Can't you just say that you used $5,000 of the borrowed funds for a few days to pay a personal bill, and pretend that the entire $20,000 was applied toward the business so that the loan is a business loan in its entirety? The answer to that question may be yes or no, depending on how you kept track of the spending. If you know the rules for tracking expenditures to debt (the *tracing rules*), you will be okay. If you don't know and apply the tracing rules, you will lose interest deductions.

MISTAKE 45
◆ Overlooking the first-in-first-out rule.

The *general* tracing rule is a *first-in-first-out* rule: For tax purposes, the proceeds of a loan that go into an account before other deposits are made to the account are treated as if they were spent *before* those other deposits. Under this first-in-first-out rule, you are in trouble with your $5,000 payment for tuition; that payment, which was made first, will be treated as made from the loan because the loan went into the account before the business receipts did. Even if you deposited $5,000 in business receipts the next day, under the general tracing rule, that tuition payment is treated as having been paid from the borrowed funds, which were deposited first. Consequently, interest on $5,000 of the loan will be nondeductible as personal interest. Not all is lost, however; there is an exception to the general rule.

MISTAKE 46
▶ Failing to spend loan proceeds on the business within thirty days.

The exception to the general tracing rule is called the *thirty-day* rule, under which you can treat the loan proceeds as having been spent on anything you choose for thirty days *after* you deposited the loan proceeds. Regardless of the order in which the expenditures were actually made, you can "trace" your choice of expenditures within the next thirty days to the loan proceeds. Therefore, using the preceding example, if you spent $20,000 on your business within thirty days after you got the loan (of which $15,000 actually came from the loan and $5,000 from the business receipt), you can choose to trace all $20,000 of business expenditures to the loan even though some of those loan proceeds were spent first on tuition. But only for thirty days. If within thirty days of getting the loan you spent only $15,000 on the business (and $5,000 on tuition), then spent another $5,000 on the business on day 31, only $15,000 could be allocated to the loan. Since $5,000 of the loan is treated under the general rule as having been spent for tuition, the interest on that $5,000 is not deductible.

MISTAKE 47
▶ **Overlooking the last-in-first-out rule.**

The importance of the thirty-day exception to the general rule becomes more apparent once you hear the rest of the general rule. Not only does the general rule say that deposits of loan proceeds are treated as spent before subsequent deposits are spent (which is arguably fair), it also says that loan proceeds are treated as spent *before* any *unborrowed* amounts that are already in the account. Which seems ridiculous. In this example, then, and still under the general rule, even if your customer had paid you $5,000 *before* you received the loan, the tuition payment, if made *after* the loan proceeds were received but before any money was spent on the business, would be treated as coming from the loan proceeds. The thirty-day rule comes to the rescue for thirty days. Regardless of the order of deposits or expenditures, any amounts spent within thirty days after the loan proceeds are deposited may, at your election, be allocated to loan proceeds or not. So you may choose to allocate to loan proceeds business expenditures made within thirty days, and make the entire loan a business loan. But if you don't make those business disbursements within thirty days, then any other disbursements made during those thirty days will be treated as if they were made from the loan (even if there was money already in the account); and if they are not business expenditures, they will reduce the amount of the loan for business purposes and the amount of the deductible interest.

Obviously, it is important to keep track of all these allocations as you make the payments. And, assuming you are always making deposits into your business account, it is important to make sure that you spend a business loan on business within thirty days after you receive it.

MISTAKE 48
▶ **Paying business debts just before you get the loan.**

These tracing rules get even sillier. The 30-day rule is applied absolutely literally: You must spend the borrowed money on business within 30 days *after* you get the loan. But what if you make the business disbursements *before* you get the loan? This is where you can get into real trouble. Back to our example. This time, your customer has paid you first. You've got $5,000, and the loan has been approved. You need to pay for business inventory *and* you need to pay the tuition. Since your suppliers are hounding you, and you know that the loan is coming through any day now, you send your suppliers $5,000. Two days later, the loan arrives, and now you pay the tuition ($5,000), and you pay your suppliers the remaining $15,000 that you owe them. How much of the loan is for business purposes? Only $15,000. Because under the thirty-day rule, you can allocate to loan proceeds only those expenditures that are made within thirty days *after* the loan proceeds are deposited to your account. Therefore, if you pay $5,000 for inventory *before* you get the loan, you pay that money from your own funds, not from borrowed funds. You can, under the thirty-day rule, allocate the rest of the business disbursements to the loan, but you've lost the interest deduction on $5,000 of the loan.

These same rules would apply if, instead of making personal expenditures, you were making investments with borrowed and unborrowed funds in your account. For noncorporate businesses, expenditures for investments must be traced just as expenditures for personal items, since the interest on any portion of a loan used to make investments is deductible only if you earn income on the investment.

MISTAKE 49
▶ Failing to maintain two accounts.

The simplest way to avoid problems with these tracing rules is to maintain two bank accounts, one for your business expenses and one for your nonbusiness expenses. If a loan is intended to be a business loan, deposit the proceeds into the business account, and don't write checks for personal items from the business account. If you have to pay the tuition, deposit your customer's payment to the personal account and write personal checks from that account.

Remember, however, that the tracing rules still apply even if you maintain two accounts. If you deposit the loan proceeds to the business account, transfer $5,000 to the personal account, then pay for the tuition, you still have used $5,000 of the loan proceeds for personal purposes. You have merely interposed an account along the way. The purpose of having two accounts is to isolate the loan proceeds in one account and to use those proceeds only for business disbursements. As long as, eventually, you spend all the isolated loan proceeds on the business, the entire loan will be considered a business loan.

MISTAKE 50
▶ **Neglecting the tracing rules in your partnership.**

Partnerships have the same tracing problems as sole proprietorships. Partnership funds are less likely to be spent on personal items, since partners are not likely to tolerate such expenditures; partnerships are more likely to run into tracing problems when borrowed funds are used for investments. The same rules apply. To the extent that expenditures for investments are traced to loans, the interest on the loans is considered investment interest which may not be deducted against the partnership's business income and which may be claimed by the partners on their own tax returns only if they have investment income (from the partnership or elsewhere).

A partnership traces its expenditures to loans just as an individual in a sole proprietorship does. Under the general rule, the first money into the account is treated as spent first; under the thirty-day exception, any expenditure made within thirty days after receiving the loan proceeds may be traced to the loan as you choose.

MISTAKE 51
▶ **Overlooking special rules for S corporations and partnerships.**

Earlier I said that if you borrowed money to put into a corporation that you owned, it was considered investment borrowing, not business borrowing, and that the interest you paid on the loan was deductible only if your investment earns income. The rule appears to be different if you borrow money to put into an S corporation in which you work actively. If you participate actively in the business activities of the S corporation, then the interest you pay on the loan is apparently deductible as business interest to the extent that the loan proceeds are used for business expenditures of the S corporation. If the proceeds are used to buy inventory, for example, or to launch a sales campaign, or to pay current bills, then the loan is viewed as a business loan and the interest is fully deductible on your own return as business interest. On the other hand, if the proceeds just sit in the corporation's account as working capital, then the loan is viewed as an investment loan. In short, you must trace the expenditures of the S corporation to the loan proceeds just as you do in your sole proprietorship. And apparently the rule is essentially the same if you borrow money to buy an S corporation: You allocate the loan proceeds among the assets of the S corporation, and, to the extent that those assets are used to run the corporation's business, the interest on the loan is business interest. Similar rules apply when you borrow money to invest in (or acquire an interest in) a partnership in which you are an active business participant.

Note that I used the word "apparently" several times in the last paragraph. The IRS has not issued clear guidelines on all these issues. Once you get to S corporations and partnerships, these interest tracing rules become too complex to handle yourself. I included them here to alert you that they exist, but you will probably need a professional tax adviser (and a clever one at that) to help you fully understand them.

Chapter Nine

Retirement Plans

Qualified pension plans are the tax-advantaged vehicles that businesspeople use to save for retirement. These are the pension and profit-sharing plans that, because they meet certain conditions set down by the tax law, provide tax advantages to employers and employees alike for retirement savings. The advantage to the employer is that he may claim a deduction at the time that he sets money aside for his employees, including himself. The advantage for the employee is that, even though money has been set aside for his benefit, he is not taxed on the money until he receives it, normally at retirement. Moreover, the money that is earned on those set-aside funds is tax-free to the employee until he receives it.

Since qualified pension plans are such a good deal for everyone, it should surprise no one that all these advantages come at a price. Before you embark on a pension program, it's important to be sure that you are prepared to pay that price.

MISTAKE 52
◆ Choosing the wrong kind of plan.

There are many kinds of qualified pension plans. The hard part is choosing the right plan for your business. Different plans are better suited for different businesses depending on the size and stability of the company and the owner's objectives for his own retirement planning. Many business owners adopt a plan that makes absolutely no sense for them because under the plan, they set aside disproportionately more money for some of their employees' retirement than they do for their own. Other owners set up plans that, it turns out, their businesses cannot afford. And some owners set up plans that don't do anybody much good. You can avoid these mistakes if you understand how different plans work.

Defined Benefit Plans

A defined benefit plan is one under which the employer first decides how much of a retirement benefit he will pay his employees and then makes contributions to the plan in amounts that will provide that benefit. He "defines" the benefit ahead of time and then sets money aside to fund it. For example, an employer may decide that he will pay each employee (including himself) a yearly retirement benefit equal to 100 percent of his final year's salary; that is, after the employee retires, and for as long as he lives, he will receive from the pension plan the same amount of money that he earned during his final year of employment. An actuary then tells the employer how much money to contribute to the plan each year so that those contributions, plus the earnings on the contributions, will provide enough money to fund this benefit once the employee does retire.

Defined Contribution Plans

In a defined contribution plan, the employer agrees simply to set aside a designated amount of money each year for each covered employee; for example, 6 percent of salary. The employer defines the *contribution*, not the *benefit*. The contributed funds are invested and earn money. Whatever is there when the employee retires is used to fund his retirement benefit. A defined contribution plan is often called a *money purchase plan* because the retirement benefit, rather than being defined in advance, depends instead on what can be purchased with the money in the plan at retirement.

In a defined benefit plan, the longer you have to fund the retirement benefit (that is, the younger and, therefore, further away from retiring the employee is), the smaller the amount of money that must be set aside now to fund it. If you are fifty years old and want to pay yourself a lifetime pension benefit of $50,000 starting in fifteen years, you obviously must set aside more money each year than if you are thirty years old and want to provide the same benefit starting in thirty-five years. Also, in a defined benefit plan, since the amount of the defined benefit usually depends on your salary, the less money you make, the smaller the amount of the annual contribution needed to fund the plan.

In a defined benefit plan, therefore, larger contributions are required for older people earning higher salaries, and smaller contributions are required for younger people earning lower salaries. In a defined contribution plan, the rate of contribution to the plan is generally the same for all employees, regardless of age. If the owner decides to set aside 6 percent of salary each year, then he funds the plan with 6 percent of his own salary and 6 percent of his employees' salaries. (Defined contribution plans may, within limits, provide larger contributions for people who have worked longer for the company, which usually means the owners.)

Which plan is right for you? If you are fifty years old and make $100,000 per year, and you have four employees in their thirties who make $30,000 per year, then with a defined benefit plan, a disproportionately large part of the contributions to that plan will be for your benefit. You have only fifteen years to fund a benefit of $100,000 for yourself, whereas you have thirty-five years to fund other retirement benefits of $30,000. On the other hand, if you have a number of employees around your age or older, in a defined benefit plan a large portion of your contributions will be used to fund their pension benefits. Unless that is your objective, you may be quite unhappy with a defined benefit plan. (When actuaries calculate what is required to fund a plan, they assume that the employer will stay in business indefinitely and that the employees will continue to work for the employer until they retire. If that actually occurs, the benefit will be fully funded. But no one really expects it to occur; and when you set up a defined benefit plan, you are not guaranteeing the defined benefit but only setting aside money at a rate that will fund the benefit if the assumptions about length of employment prove valid.)

In a defined contribution plan, as long as you are the highest-paid person in your company, the absolute amount of money set aside will be larger for you than for any employee even if you are younger than some of your employees. However, if you have a large number of employees, your total contributions to the plan for their combined benefit will be hefty—contributions that might have been allocated more toward funding your own retirement if you had instead chosen a defined benefit plan.

So there are no pat answers, and usually you need a pension plan expert to recommend a plan for you. The mistake to avoid is being uninformed and choosing a plan that diverts most of your business profits to your employees' retirement funds—unless that is what you set out to do.

MISTAKE 53
♦ Underestimating the cost of your retirement plan.

Retirement plans can become expensive. In fact, depending on the type of plan you have, they can become ruinous. If it turns out that your business cannot afford its retirement plan, you may be in a no-win situation: If you continue to fund the plan, your business goes broke; if you stop funding the plan too soon, the IRS assesses back taxes or penalties. Before you set up a plan, therefore, know what it is going to cost you.

In a defined benefit plan, once you define the benefit, you have to set aside the money every year to fund it. If your business suffers a downturn, the money needed to meet the yearly funding requirement may not be there.

Defined benefit plans can also end up costing more than you expected. When an actuary decides how much money your business must contribute to a defined benefit plan, he assumes that the plan will earn a certain amount of money each year. If he's wrong about the earnings, you have to make up the difference. If your actuary assumes that the funds in the plan will earn 5 percent per year, but for several years they earn only 4 percent per year, the plan's poorer-than-expected investment return will mean that, in order to fund the defined benefit, larger employer contributions will be required to offset the poor investment results. In a defined benefit plan, therefore, you bear the investment risk; however, you also reap the investment rewards. If the plan's investment results are better than expected, smaller employer contributions will be required in later years.

If your defined benefit plan becomes "underfunded," because, for example, of poor investment results, your business must make up the difference. Otherwise, the IRS assesses your business a penalty equal to 10 percent of the amount of the shortfall (100 percent if you don't correct the problem quickly).

Accordingly, defined benefit plans are best suited for stable companies in stable industries that are likely to be able to make the contributions required.

In a defined contribution plan, the contribution is always a percentage of salary, so you have a better idea of what your business's yearly contributions will be. But don't forget that as salaries increase so do the pension plan contributions. Employees pushing for raises aren't always sympathetic to the fact that not only do you have to pay them more salary, but you have to make larger pension plan contributions for them as well.

The desire by employers to gain control over the contributions they are required to make to their pension plans is addressed by another kind of plan—the *profit-sharing plan*. In a profit-sharing plan, the employer is required to set aside money for the employees' retirement each year *only* if it has profits. Thus, the plan might say that 7 percent of the employer's profits (or, assuming there are profits, 7 percent of sales or of net sales) for the year will be put into the retirement fund, to be allocated among the employees in proportion to their salaries. If your company doesn't have profits in a particular year, it doesn't have to make contributions to the retirement plan for that year. Indeed, in a profit-sharing plan, the employer can even change the formula from year to year; it can decide to contribute 7 percent of profits in one year and 5 percent of profits the next year.

Profits that are contributed to the plan each year can be allocated among the employees who participate in the plan according to the kinds of formulas used for defined contribution plans. Therefore, allocations among the employees may be based on a straight percentage of salary or on a combination of salary and years of employment (for example, 4 percent of salary for two years of service, 5 percent for three years of service, and so on).

Profit-sharing plans are obviously very attractive to employers who are uncertain of their ability to fund a plan every year or who want the flexibility to raise or lower their contributions to the plan, and these plans have become quite popular. The flexibility comes at a price, however; in a profit-sharing plan, the total amount of contributions to the plan that can be deducted by the employer each year for all employees covered by the plan cannot exceed 15 percent of the total compensation of those employees. Therefore, if you had a very good year and your contribution formula resulted in everyone (including yourself) enjoying a contribution equal to 20 percent of their salary, only 75 percent of that contribution would be deductible. (The nondeductible portion of the contribution can be carried over to another year and, subject to the same limitations, deducted in that later year.) Thus, with a profit-sharing plan, you can limit your obligation to make contributions in a bad year, but you also limit your ability to shelter profits in a good year.

Another kind of plan that gives you some control of the contributions required to be made to the plan is a *target benefit plan*, which is a combination of a defined benefit and a defined contribution plan. Like a defined benefit plan, a target benefit plan defines the benefit that it intends to pay (the targeted benefit). Unlike a defined benefit plan, it does not guarantee that benefit if the actuarial assumptions prove to be incorrect. If investment results are poorer than expected, the employer does not increase his contributions to the plan to offset the lower investment return; if investment results are better than expected, he does not reduce his contributions to the plan. Like the defined contribution plan, therefore, the final benefit depends on what is in the plan when the employee retires. The employer aims for a targeted benefit, but sometimes misses the target.

The advantage of the target benefit plan is that it permits you to make larger contributions for yourself if you are the oldest employee, without taking the investment risk of a defined benefit plan. The disadvantage is that you are obligated to fund the targeted benefit through good times and bad, and you get no relief from making contributions even if investment results are good.

MISTAKE 54
▶ **Overestimating the amount of contributions that you can make.**

The tax savings available through qualified retirement plans are not unlimited. In order to be qualified, a retirement plan must cap the amount of retirement benefits that can be set aside each year by the employer — often referred to as "limiting the accrual of benefits." The important thing for the owner of a business to understand is that these caps on plan contributions tend to reduce the amount of contributions that can be made for higher-income earners, that is, the owner of the business, not the lower-paid people who work for him. The limitations on accrual of benefits are different for different kinds of plans, as follows.

The maximum amount of money that may be contributed to a defined benefit plan on behalf of an individual is the amount needed to fund a benefit equal to the individual's average compensation during his three best years of employment. Thus, if your company has a defined benefit plan that promises to pay your employees 100 percent of their salary in their last full year of employment, and if your final year's salary is projected to be $80,000 but your average compensation for your three best years with your company is projected to be $70,000, you can set aside only as much money as is needed to fund a retirement benefit of $70,000. Most business owners can live with that limitation. It's another limitation that is irksome and often catches them by surprise: In no event can the plan fund for a benefit in excess of about $105,000. (This limitation increases each year with inflation.) Even if you are making $200,000 per year with your company, the greatest annual retirement benefit your plan can fund is $105,000. If you have other employees earning $105,000, the benefit you fund for yourself will be no greater than the benefit you fund for them.

The maximum amount of money that may be contributed to a defined contribution plan (which includes a target benefit plan and a profit-sharing plan) on behalf of an individual in the plan is $30,000 or, if less, 25 percent of that individual's compensation for the year. (The $30,000 limitation also increases with inflation.) There is one additional limitation in calculating contributions to defined contribution plans: The most compensation that can be taken into account in determining the contribution is about $160,000 (a figure that also increases each year with inflation). Therefore, if your employee makes $30,000 per year and you make $300,000, and you contribute 10 percent of pay to your plan, you contribute $3,000 for your employee and $16,000 (10% of $160,000), not $30,000, for yourself.

For self-employed people (sole proprietors and partners in a partnership), the 25 percent limitation is actually smaller because, in calculating this limitation, a self-employed person must reduce his compensation by the amount of the contribution he makes to the plan—a circular mathematical formula that results in an effective limitation of 13.04 percent of total compensation.

Do not confuse limitations on the accrual of benefits with limitations on deductible contribution. If the plan does not provide for limitations on the accrual of benefits, it is not a qualified plan, and no contributions for it are deductible. So the limitations on accrual of benefits will always be in your plan. If the plan is qualified, all contributions to it, credited in accordance with the terms of the plan, will be deductible—except, as we have seen, for profit-sharing plans deductible contributions cannot exceed 15 percent of compensation (and nondeductible contributions can be carried over to future years).

MISTAKE 55
▶ **Terminating your plan soon after starting it.**

You might think that if your plan proves to be too expensive or doesn't seem to be delivering the benefits that you expected, you will simply stop making contributions to it, that is, cancel it. But you don't always have that option. Your pension plan is supposed to be a "plan," a term that connotes a certain duration. If you discontinue a plan too quickly, the IRS might decide that it was never a plan to begin with and disqualify it for all the years that you had it. If, for example, you had a plan for just three years and then discontinued it, the IRS might claim that you never really had a plan and that all those contributions to the plan were actually wages that you paid to your employees. It would then assess your business for payroll taxes and charge you and your other employees with income equal to the contributions you made to the plan on your and their behalf. You will have a lot of unhappy employees, yourself included. So it's not advisable to start a plan unless you understand it and are comfortable that you will be able to keep it going.

MISTAKE 56
▶ **Letting your plan become disqualified.**

Losing your plan's qualified status because you did not maintain it long enough or for other reasons is disastrous. For one thing, the plan's income will no longer be tax-exempt, and up to 40 percent of that income will be used to pay federal taxes, leaving less money for your employees' retirement and some very unhappy employees (who may sue you). Second, deductions for your contributions to the plan will be disallowed to the extent your employees are not vested in their plan benefits. If your employees are vested in their benefits, your contributions to the plan will be considered wages, subject to payroll taxes. Finally, your employees will be taxed for all vested benefits that accrue during the period that the plan is disqualified, even if they can't get their hands on the benefits to pay the taxes that become due.

Worse, plan disqualifications are often retroactive because it takes the IRS a few years to audit your plan and determine that it is disqualified and has been for several years. Now the list of horribles goes back several years: The plan owes back taxes with interest; your company is liable for payroll taxes that were never withheld; your employees owe years of taxes for income that they don't have. And their lawyers are saying that it's all your fault. Once you have a pension plan, be sure to use a pension plan expert to help you keep your plan qualified.

MISTAKE 57
‣ **Engaging in financial transactions with your plan.**

Employers who establish retirement plans must be cautious about engaging in transactions with their plans. Employers (and people related to employers, such as the owner of a company that is the employer) are prohibited from lending money to a plan or borrowing from it, buying property from a plan or selling property to it, or engaging in practically any other financial transaction with a plan. There is a reason for prohibitions on such transactions: Once a pension plan has been in existence for a while, large sums of money start to accumulate in it, and an employer with a cash flow problem may become tempted to borrow money from the plan. Such a transaction is nearly always prohibited.

If an employer engages in a prohibited transaction with his plan, he suffers two sanctions: First, he has to undo the transaction; second, the IRS imposes a penalty on the employer equal to 5 percent of the amount of the transaction for each year until the transaction is undone. So if your company borrowed $100,000 from its pension plan in 1996, and the IRS detected the prohibited borrowing in 1999, and you repaid the money in that year (with interest), the penalty would be $20,000. If you do not undo the transaction within ninety days after the IRS tells you to, the penalty is 100 percent.

Never engage in any kind of transaction with your company's plan without first seeking the advice of a pension expert. Even transactions that are intended to benefit the plan are prohibited. One employer, an automobile dealer, gave all his new-car loan business to the plan — a very lucrative business that enabled the plan to earn far more money than it would have through more traditional investments. The employer was nonetheless penalized for engaging in a prohibited transaction with his plan and forced to place all the loans somewhere else.

Chapter Ten

S Corporations

S corporations are real corporations under state law and provide you with all the protection of a real corporation. They act as a shield against your business creditors (assuming you have not guaranteed the corporation's debts). But S corporations are mostly disregarded for tax purposes. You pay tax on the corporation's profits (or deduct the corporation's losses) as though you were running the business as a sole proprietorship. You figure the corporation's net profits or losses, and you carry that figure to the front of your individual income tax return, adding it to (or subtracting it from) the rest of your income.

With their special status, it should come as no surprise that S corporations, in order to be recognized as such, must comply with a number of specific rules. Nor should it come as a surprise that these rules frequently get S corporation owners into trouble.

MISTAKE 58
> **Failing to properly elect S corporation treatment.**

You don't have to be a rocket scientist to make an S corporation election. The IRS provides a form — Form 2553 — which is titled Election to Be Taxed as an S Corporation. It's one page long, seeks information about the corporation and its shareholders, and takes about ten minutes to complete. The form must be completed accurately, however; otherwise, you don't have an S corporation.

The most frequent mistake people make in the S corporation election process is failing to have all the shareholders of the corporation consent to the election. Form 2553 has a section that calls for the identities and signatures of all the shareholders. If you leave one shareholder off the list, or one doesn't sign the form indicating consent, you don't have an S corporation. The IRS may discover six years later that one of your shareholders didn't sign Form 2553, at which point it disallows S corporation status from the beginning.

Sometimes a defect in your election will appear on the face of the form, and then the IRS will send the form back to you, rejecting your S corporation election. For example, the form asks about classes of stock, and if you indicate that your S corporation has two classes, without making it clear that those classes differ only in voting rights, then the IRS will reject the S corporation election.

A rejection of a defective election is not the end of

the world; you simply refile a corrected form. However, several weeks will pass before the IRS reviews the original form and returns it to you. And by then it may be too late to make an S corporation election for the year you desired to—a subject we turn to next.

MISTAKE 59
▶ **Waiting too long to make the S corporation election.**

An election to treat your corporation as an S corporation starting with a particular tax year must be made no later than the fifteenth day of the third month of that tax year (unless you can demonstrate to the IRS that you had reasonable cause for making the election after the required date). If your corporation's year begins on January 1, and you want it to become an S corporation for that year, you must file Form 2553 by March 15. If your corporation's tax year begins on September 1, you must file Form 2553 by November 15. Many people say that you have seventy-five days to make an S corporation election, but for most companies, that is not true. A corporation that is on a calendar year has only seventy-four days in which to elect S corporation status, except for leap years.

If Form 2553 is filed after the fifteenth day of the third month, your corporation's election as an S corporation is effective for the following year. Indeed, you can file Form 2553 for the following year at any time during the current year, and the election will be effective for the following year.

While the election to become an S corporation

doesn't have to be filed until seventy-four days into the year, it's a mistake to wait until the last minute. S corporation elections should be filed as early as possible because if for some reason the IRS rejects the election, you will still have time to refile it. If you want your S corporation election to be effective for the current calendar year and you file Form 2553 on March 1 without a shareholder signature, the IRS will return it to you around April 1 — too late to make the election for the current year. Had you filed the form in January, or even during the previous year, you would have had time before the March 15 filing deadline to correct any mistakes that you made.

New corporations that desire to be S corporations must also file Form 2553 within two months and 15 days after the beginning of their tax year, but for new corporations it can be difficult to determine when the tax year begins. Obviously, you are safe if you file within two months and fifteen days of incorporating your corporation. If you are unsure about whether you want S corporation status at that time, you may be able to wait, but you are taking a chance. The IRS says that a new corporation's tax year begins when it acquires shareholders, when it acquires assets, or when it begins to engage in a business, whichever occurs first. The time at which your corporation acquires shareholders may depend on state law where you live. The mere fact of incorporation does not mean that the corporation has shareholders; but if you are treating a corporation as your own even though you haven't actually issued stock yet, shareholders may exist for tax purposes. If your attorney is holding a corporation on the "shelf" for you until you decide whether you need it, you may have time. If you are unsure about whether to make a new corporation an S corporation, it is probably advisable not to form the corporation until you have made up your mind. Many people starting a new business figure they must have a corporation right away, when, in fact, you can probably go a long way in planning your new business before actually forming your corporation.

MISTAKE 60
 ● **Failing to qualify as an S corporation.**

Not every corporation is permitted to be an S corporation. To qualify, a corporation must meet several criteria, both within its first year as an S corporation and at all times thereafter. In most cases, these requirements are easy enough to meet, as long as you know what they are. Frequently, problems arise because the owner or owners of the S corporation are not aware of these requirements and don't even realize that their corporations cannot qualify as S corporations or that they have lost their status as S corporations. We cover these criteria next.

● *Only individuals and their estates, certain trusts, and other S corporations may be shareholders.* An S corporation must be owned by human beings. If one of those human beings dies, his estate may continue to own stock in the S corporation. Certain trusts that benefit individuals may also own stock in S corporations. And other S corporations may own stock in S corporations as long as they own all of the stock. But only these kinds of shareholders are permitted. That means that partnerships cannot be shareholders in an S corporation. Neither can corporations other than other S corporations, pension plans, or individual retirement accounts, nor any other entity that you can think of. Only individuals, estates, certain trusts, and other S corporations. If an S corporation has any impermissible shareholders, it doesn't qualify as an S corporation, and it will not be treated as an S corporation for tax purposes.

- *No nonresident alien shareholders.* All shareholders of an S corporation must be U.S. citizens or residents. Nonresident aliens are not permitted because the income of an S corporation is taxed at the shareholder level, and the IRS fears that if a nonresident alien owns stock in an S corporation, he won't pay tax on his share of the corporation's profits. One importer of home furnishings, in order to give a key foreign supplier a small stake in his business, sold 2 percent of the stock in his S corporation to the supplier. Three years later, he learned from the IRS that his S corporation status had evaporated on the day of the sale.

- *A maximum of seventy-five shareholders.* S corporations may not have more than seventy-five shareholders. The instant they acquire a seventy-sixth shareholder, they lose their status as S corporations. Very few corporations violate this rule inadvertently, since if you have seventy-five shareholders, one of them is bound to be aware of it.

- *One class of stock.* An S corporation may have

only one class of stock—although there is one exception to this rule: An S corporation may have more than one class of stock if the only characteristic that distinguishes the different classes is voting rights. For example, you can give key employees or investors a stake in your corporation but still totally control your corporation by giving them nonvoting common stock. They have all the rights that you have in the corporation, but they can't vote their stock.

This one-class-of-stock requirement is usually violated when you need an investor in your corporation who wants greater rights than you in the corporation's profits. Because he wants his investment to be repaid before you take dividends out of your corporation, he asks for preferred stock. If you give him preferred stock—or any kind of stock that grants him a preference in the assets or income of your corporation—your S corporation status terminates immediately.

S corporation owners who know about the one-class-of-stock requirement still manage to jeopardize their S corporation status by looking for ways around the requirement. For example, they provide an investor with a note that must be repaid before earnings are distributed to the other owners. Depending on how these transactions are structured, the IRS may come in and treat the note as a second class of stock, and disqualify the S corporation. So whenever you are giving a lender or an investor rights in your corporation that smack of an equity interest, it is advisable to seek professional advice first.

MISTAKE 61
▶ Letting your S corporation's status slip away.

These qualification requirements for S corporations must be met when the corporation elects to be treated as an S corporation and they must be met each day thereafter. One corporation elected to be an S corporation at a time when it had a second class of stock. In the following year, it eliminated the second class of stock. Many years later when the IRS found the initial invalidity, it disqualified the corporation as an S corporation in the initial year, in the following year, and for all the subsequent years. The fact that the corporation had eliminated its second class of stock in the second year did not make it a qualified S corporation in subsequent years because it wasn't a qualified S corporation at the time that it elected S corporation status. The election was never valid in the first place. Another corporation started out as a qualified S corporation, then issued a second class of stock in the next year, then eliminated it later that year. It lost its S corporation status in the year in which it issued (and eliminated) the second class of stock and for each year thereafter. You have to start out qualified; otherwise your corporation is not an S corporation to begin with. And you have to stay qualified; once your corporation loses its qualified status, it cannot regain it by eliminating the problem that disqualified it. And note, once a corporation loses its S status, it cannot normally become an S corporation again for five years.

MISTAKE 62

◗ Failing to promptly correct an inadvertent disqualification of your S corporation.

If your S corporation fails to properly elect its status or loses its status inadvertently, the IRS can permit you to make amends, but IRS agents don't always tell you that. It's an initiative that you must take on your own. Also, if you determine on your own that your S corporation has lost its qualified status, you must seek to make amends immediately, not wait for an IRS agent to discover the mistake. You are permitted to make amends if the IRS is satisfied that the termination of S corporation status was indeed inadvertent, and that you took immediate steps to correct the problem causing the loss of status (you must also agree to tax adjustments for the period during which S corporation status was lost). Thus, if a small shareholder transferred his stock in your S corporation to another corporation, your S corporation would lose its S status on the day of the transfer. But if you could show the IRS that you didn't know about the transfer (and would have had no reason to know about it), and if you get that stock back into an individual's hands as soon as possible, the IRS would be likely to permit your corporation to regain its S status as soon as you had repaired the damage. Acting quickly once you discover the problem seems to be the most important criterion used by the IRS in deciding to forgive inadvertent losses of S status. The fact that it takes a long time to discover the problem is not fatal (assuming there wasn't any reason for you to have been aware of it), as long as you address the problem as soon as you do discover it.

MISTAKE 63
▶ **Failing to have sufficient basis in your S corporation to claim its losses on your tax return.**

There are two main reasons for having an S corporation: to prevent taxation of business income at the corporate level and to claim business losses on your own tax return. We looked at the corporate-level tax problem in Chapter 4 when we examined salaries, dividends, and loans. The S corporation makes those issues go away: You are taxed on the profits of your S corporation as though you were running the business as a sole proprietorship, so in most cases, it doesn't matter how you take money out of your S corporation (we look at one exception shortly).

S corporation shareholders can also claim the losses of their corporations on their own tax returns. If your corporation loses $20,000 for the year (and you are the only shareholder), you get a deduction on your own tax return of $20,000. If a corporation has more than one shareholder, then all the shareholders divide the losses proportionately. The ability to claim S corporation losses on their own returns is the primary motive for many businesspeople to seek S corporation status. The losses suffered during the start-up phase of a business can be used to reduce the tax liabilities of the owners. Once the business starts to earn profits, you can continue with an S corporation if you want to avoid corporate-level tax, or you can revoke your S corporation status if it is to your advantage to have a regular corporation.

There's just one catch, and it is frequently overlooked. The amount of loss that you can claim from an S corporation in any year is limited to your "basis" in the corporation for the year. If the corporation has a loss of $20,000 but your basis is only $10,000, you can claim only $10,000 in losses on your own tax return. Getting basis in an S corporation is an area in which many people make mistakes — usually because of the way they borrow money for their business.

Determining your basis in an S corporation for purposes of claiming losses is not a simple exercise, but it starts with how much you put into the corporation as capital and how much you lend to the corporation. Your initial basis in an S corporation is the sum of your capital contributions to the corporation and your loans to the corporation. If you capitalize your corporation with $10,000 and lend it $10,000, your basis is $20,000. You can claim on your own tax return up to $20,000 in S corporation losses.

People end up with less basis in their S corporations than they expected once they start to borrow from a bank. Money that an S corporation borrows from a bank does not give its shareholder basis. If you capitalize your corporation with $10,000 and your corporation borrows $10,000 from a bank (or from your brother-in-law), your basis is $10,000; even if your corporation spends all $20,000 and has a $20,000 loss for the year, you can deduct only $10,000 of those losses.

From a financial standpoint, it may make sense to have the corporation borrow from the bank instead of from you. If the corporation is going to lose money, let it lose someone else's money. But few banks will let you off that easily. If the bank makes you guarantee the loan to the corporation, then you are still financially responsible for the loan, but you don't get any basis from the loan. Only when you pay off on your guarantee does a bank loan give you basis in the corporation. If you are responsible for the loan, then you might as well get basis from it so that you can deduct losses against it. Accordingly, often the way to finance an S corporation with debt is to borrow the money yourself from the bank, then lend it to your corporation. You get basis in the corporation from the money that you lend it, even if you have just borrowed that money from someone else.

Your basis in your S corporation goes up and down as time goes by and things happen. It is increased by the corporation's taxable income that you pay tax on and reduced by losses that you claim. It goes up when you put more money into the corporation and goes down as you withdraw money from the corporation. After your corporation has turned a profit, the amount of your basis becomes less important because you will not have any more losses to claim. After that, basis becomes important again only when you sell the corporation and need to determine your capital gain or loss.

MISTAKE 64
> ◆ Not being an "active participant" in your S corporation.

Many people think that they can enjoy the losses generated by an S corporation simply by investing in an S corporation. Not true. S corporation shareholders can claim losses from the S corporation against other business income (including salary) or dividend or interest income (or capital gains) only if they work for the S corporation or at least participate actively in its day-to-day affairs. If you are a "passive" investor, you can claim S corporation losses only against "passive" income, that is, income from investments in other S corporations or partnerships or limited liability companies. The losses of an S corporation in which you are a passive investor cannot be claimed against your salary or against your investment income, only against income from other businesses in which you have a passive role.

MISTAKE 65
> ◆ Going overboard on reducing your salary from an S corporation to save payroll taxes.

As a shareholder in an S corporation, you may take money out of the corporation in the same three ways that you take it out of a regular corporation: as salary, as dividends, or as a loan. As an S corporation shareholder, however, you don't much care how you withdraw money — at least not from the standpoint of *income taxes*, because you pay income tax on all of the corporation's income anyway.

As payroll taxes increase, however, the manner in which you withdraw money from an S corporation becomes more important from the viewpoint of *payroll taxes*. If you pay yourself a salary of $60,000, you pay income tax on the entire salary, and you and your corporation also pay a payroll tax on the entire salary (a combined payroll tax rate, as explained in Chapter 2, of 15.3 percent). Since it is all your money anyway, why not pay yourself a salary of $30,000 and take a $30,000 dividend? You save $4,590 in payroll taxes ($30,000 × 15.3 percent). In fact, why not work for your corporation for no salary and save $9,180 in payroll taxes?

The IRS monitors this practice among S corporations. Just as it wants part of your salary to be a dividend if you own a regular corporation, so it wants your pay from your S corporation — at least up to the wage base — to be subject to payroll taxes. If you pay your secretary $30,000 per year, you will probably not get away with paying yourself $30,000 per year, as well. As a practical matter, the IRS will try to force you to treat all payments up to the wage base as salary.

The real contest comes with payments above the wage base. Recall from Chapter 2 that salary payments above the wage base are taxed at a combined rate of 2.9 percent. As the numbers grow, this tax becomes significant. If you make $300,000 from your S corporation, the 2.9 percent payroll tax on wages above $60,000 comes to nearly $7,000. When are you safe calling those payments dividends rather than wages? This problem is a relatively new one (because the 2.9 percent tax is relatively new), and even the experts are not sure of the answer. No doubt, "reasonable" salaries in the S corporation context will be judged in the same manner as in the regular corporation context (see Chapter 4), except that each side will be arguing for the opposite result.

MISTAKE 66
◆ Overlooking the restrictions on fringe benefits in an S corporation.

There is one disadvantage to an S corporation that many people don't learn of until they decide to use an S corporation: Shareholders who own 2 percent or more of the corporation ("2-percent shareholders") cannot enjoy certain of the tax-free benefits that other employees enjoy. If you have a regular corporation and you sponsor an accident and health insurance plan for your employees (including yourself), the premiums that you pay for this insurance are deductible to the corporation and tax-free to the employees, including yourself. In the case of S corporations, however, those premiums are not tax-free to 2-percent shareholders. The 2-percent shareholders must include in their income the premiums that the corporation pays on their behalf. The same is true for many other fringe benefits, as well. For example, if the S corporation provides group term life insurance to its employees, the 2-percent shareholder must include the premium for his life insurance as income.

Self-insured medical reimbursement plans and cafeteria plans are covered by the same rule. If the corporation were a regular corporation, the shareholder-employees could receive these benefits tax-free, as do the other employees.

The reason for this special treatment of certain fringe benefits presumably lies in the fact that the S corporation is claiming a deduction for the cost of these benefits — a deduction reflected in the shareholder's share of the corporation's profit or losses — and the shareholder should not, therefore, enjoy the tax benefit twice. The problem with this rationale is that not all fringe benefits are treated in this manner; the value of working condition fringe benefits, qualified employee discounts, educational assistance programs, dependent care assistance programs, and other fringe benefits are tax-free, even to 2-percent shareholders.

START-UP SITUATIONS

MISTAKE 67
▶ **Failing to analyze whether you want (or want to keep) an S corporation.**

When do you want an S corporation? It would be convenient if there were always a simple answer to this question, but usually there isn't.

Partnership or S Corporation?

Since the tax consequences are essentially the same in a partnership and an S corporation, the decision to use either structure is usually a business decision, not a tax decision. If you want the protection of the corporate shield — from business debts or liability — you would choose an S corporation. If you are unconcerned about business debts and can insure against liability, you may not need a corporation.

If you have business associates and you and your associates intend to have different rights in the business, an S corporation may not be suitable for you since S corporations can have only one class of stock, whereas in a partnership you may make any agreements among yourselves that you want on the division of profits. Likewise, if you intend to reward your employees with preferred stock, an S corporation will not work.

Generally, a partnership is a more flexible business entity than an S corporation, simply because it is not subject to all the restrictions imposed on the qualification of an S corporation.

S Corporation or Regular Corporation?

If you are determined to have a corporation, then at least when you are starting out, an S corporation is probably preferable. Your ability to deduct your business's start-up losses will probably outweigh any of the inconveniences of operating as an S corporation (and, when you are starting out, things like preferred

stock or participating debt are usually not under consideration). Also, if necessary, you can always terminate your corporation's S status.

ONGOING BUSINESS

As your business grows, however, the S corporation
may not be so clearly preferable, and you may wish to
revert to regular corporation status. While the typi-
cal line of reasoning is that it is better to pay tax one
time at the shareholder level (that is, as an S corporation) than at both the corporate and the shareholder
levels, this reasoning can be faulty. Particularly in
growing businesses, S corporation owners often find
themselves strapped for cash to pay the taxes,
because the profits have been put back into the business. If your S corporation has $500,000 in profits,
you pay tax on all $500,000 even if, because you
reinvested $200,000 in the business, you only drew
out $300,000 in cash. Under those circumstances,
you might have left $200,000 in the corporation, tax-
able at a corporate rate of about 30 percent instead of
an individual rate of nearly 40 percent. Many S corporation owners are rich people on paper but can
barely pay the rent.

The choice between a regular and an S corporation also depends on the nature of your business
expenditures. If most of those expenditures are
currently deductible, an S corporation might be
suitable because the profits that you pay tax on are
reduced by the expenditures. But if your business
requires plants and machinery, you will find yourself

depreciating large cash expenditures over many years, and there may not be enough cash to pay the taxes on the business.

The nature of your business itself also affects your choice of corporation. Service businesses and retail establishments are often more suitable for S corporations because you get paid as you perform the work. But if you are a wholesaler, with large sums tied up in inventory and receivables, cash may be a problem at tax time.

So there are no easy answers. Before you make a decision, you will probably have to consult with someone — an accountant, a tax attorney, or a business consultant — who has seen businesses like yours before and who can surmise what will happen. It is always easier the second, third, or fourth time around, and you would be well advised to talk to someone who has done it before.

Chapter Eleven

Owning More than One Business

Multiple business ownership is quite common. A person who owns an automobile dealership might also own a finance company. Someone who owns a construction company might also own a real estate brokerage firm. Many physicians own medical equipment leasing companies. Stockbrokers own restaurants. The manner in which the ownership of multiple businesses is structured can have enormous income tax consequences. Unfortunately, many businesspeople do not consider these consequences until it is too late.

MISTAKE 68
► **Owning more than one business without a holding company.**

The failure to structure business ownership properly is one of the most common mistakes businesspeople make. In one case a person owned two corporations: one of these corporations had huge profits on which taxes were paid every year; the other regularly suffered losses, which did the owner no good whatsoever. In fact in one year, the total net income from the two companies was $200,000, and the total tax liability for the two companies was also $200,000. Why? Because one company had profits of nearly $600,000 and the other company had losses of $400,000, but the profits of the first company could not be reduced by the losses of the second. At the end of the day, only the government made money from the businesses.

Whenever possible, business organizations should be structured so that the profits of one business can be offset by the losses of the other. But unless all your companies are S corporations (a subject we return to shortly), there is only one way to do that: when the multiple companies can file a *consolidated tax return*.

A consolidated tax return is just what its name implies: It is a form on which the returns of more than one corporation have been consolidated into one return. The taxable income (or loss) of one corporation is determined in one column; the taxable income (or loss) of a second corporation is determined in another column; and so on. After the taxable incomes (or losses) of all the corporations have been determined, they are netted one against the other, and the result is the taxable income (or loss) of the "consolidated group" of corporations. In practice, it is not quite that simple because certain intercompany adjustments must be made; nevertheless, the result is just about that simple.

If two corporations file a consolidated return, therefore, and one corporation has profits of $200,000 and the other has losses of $100,000, the taxable income of the consolidated group is $100,000, and that is the figure on which taxes are paid. The losses of the loss corporation reduce the profits of the profitable corporation.

If you have more than one corporation, and one or more of them loses money, filing a consolidated return usually makes an enormous amount of sense (still assuming that these corporations are not S corporations). But not every company may file a consolidated return.

A consolidated return can be filed only by corporations that have one of two specifically defined relationships to one another:

1. The corporations are all subsidiaries of the same parent (that is, "brother-sister" corporations), and the parent is a corporation.
2. The corporations all have a parent-subsidiary relationship to one another (i.e., a "vertical chain" of corporations).

If two corporations are both owned by the same individual (that is, they are brother-sister corporations but they do not have a common parent that is a corporation), they cannot file consolidated returns. In order to file consolidated returns, therefore, when you have brother-sister corporations, you need to have a holding company between you and your operating corporations. You own all the stock of your holding company, and your holding company owns all the stock of your other corporations. Now the first condition is met, and your holding company and your operating companies can file a consolidated return, and the profits of one company can be offset by the losses of the other.

If you own your operating corporations in a vertical chain—you own one company that in turn owns another company, and so on—then the second condition is met and all these corporations can file consolidated returns. You do not need a holding company when your corporations are in a vertical chain because the corporation at the top of the chain owns (directly or through the other corporations in the chain) the rest of the companies.

There may be times when you don't want your operating companies to file a consolidated return. A consolidated return will be disadvantageous if both (or all) of your corporations have small amounts of earnings and would pay less tax if they filed separate returns. For example, if each of your two corporations had profits of $50,000 and filed separate returns, each would pay a tax of $7,500, for a total tax of $15,000. If they filed a consolidated return, showing total profits of $100,000, the total tax would be $22,250—because the corporate tax rates go up as the consolidated income rises. However, since corporate income above $75,000 is taxed at a flat rate of 34 percent, consolidated returns are disadvantageous only when total income is relatively low.

The fact that you may not want to file a consolidated return does not mean that you should not have a structure that permits you to do so, for even if you have a structure that permits filing a consolidated return, you are not obligated to do so; you can use a consolidated filing only if and when it benefits you.

MISTAKE 69

▶ **Assuming that the losses of one
S corporation will always offset the
profits of another S corporation.**

S corporations cannot file consolidated returns. (S corporations, you may recall, cannot be owned by other corporations.) However, the profits of one S corporation can *sometimes*, not always, be reduced by the losses of another S corporation. It is the "not always" part that surprises many business owners. When you own an S corporation, you report the profits of that corporation on your own return and pay the tax on those profits yourself. If your S corporation suffers losses, you can claim those losses on your own return. Therefore, if you own two S corporations and one has profits and the other losses, you can in effect offset the profits of one with the losses of the other — because the profits and the losses are carried to your own return and netted against one another.

Here's the catch: You can claim the losses of an S corporation on your own return *only if you have sufficient basis in the S corporation* (see Chapter 10). If you don't have sufficient basis in the loss corporation, you cannot claim the loss — and the fact that you have another S corporation with profits does not change that fact. Whether you can claim on your own return the loss of an S corporation depends *solely* on whether you have enough basis in the loss corporation; it does not in any way depend on whether you also have profits from another S corporation. So if you don't have enough basis in the loss corporation, you pay taxes on the profits from the profitable corporation and get no benefit from the losses of the loss corporation.

Until recently, there was no way around this problem, except to terminate your S corporations' status and have your companies file consolidated returns. Now there is a solution, however; you can make one S corporation the wholly owned subsidiary of the other S corporation. For tax purposes, the two S corporations are then treated as one corporation whose taxable income is the net income of both entities. If you have two S corporations and one makes money and one loses money, it's a mistake not to restructure them as a parent and a subsidiary.

MISTAKE 70
▶ **Overcharging or undercharging one of your companies.**

When you own more than one company and your companies do business with one another, the opportunity exists to shift profits from one corporation to another through intercompany transactions. For example, if your construction company had net operating loss carryovers that could be used to shield other income from taxes, it might pay your real estate brokerage firm a commission of 4 percent for selling the houses that it built, instead of the standard 6 percent commission; by doing so, it lowers its costs and retains more of its profits and then reduces those profits with its loss carryovers. You might also try to keep income in the construction company at the expense of the brokerage firm if your construction company was in the 15 percent tax bracket and your brokerage company was in the 34 percent bracket.

Multiple business ownership gives you the capability to shift profits between businesses, and you should take advantage of it, but not in a willy-nilly fashion. The IRS watches for intercompany transactions fairly carefully; if it audits one of your corporations, it will ask for a schedule of intercompany transactions and then audit the other company. And it requires your companies to deal with one another at arm's length. If your brokerage firm sold your construction company's homes for a 4 percent commission, the IRS would want proof that an unrelated brokerage firm would have done the same thing. It is entirely possible that if given the opportunity to sell all your houses, an unrelated firm might have been happy to charge you only 4 percent, but you need to determine that when you are setting the intercompany commission, not when the agent begins his audit. If you cannot satisfy the agent that the intercompany transaction is at arm's length, then he will adjust the incomes of both companies to reflect an arm's-length transaction. So intercompany transactions can be used to shift profits between corporations, but if the price of the transaction is outside the market price, you must be able to justify the departure from the norm.

MISTAKE 71
▸ **Overpaying payroll taxes when you own more than one corporation.**

When you own more than one business and operate your businesses through separate corporations, you may end up paying higher payroll taxes if you work for each corporation. The reason: Every employer is liable for his share of the social security tax on each employee, no matter how many employers the employee has.

Payroll taxes were examined in Chapter 2. One of those taxes—the social security tax—is imposed on both the employer and the employee. Each party pays a tax of 7.65 percent on the wage base and a tax of 1.45 percent on all wages above the wage base. If you are employed by one corporation and earn a salary of $120,000, that corporation pays about $5,600 in social security taxes from its own funds (apart from the social security taxes that it withholds from your paycheck).

If you are employed by two employers, the social security tax applies to both. If you owned two corporations and paid yourself a salary of $60,000 from each of them, each would pay $4,590 in social security taxes from its own funds. Total social security tax payments from the two corporations: $9,180, compared to $5,600 when you worked for one company for $120,000. The $3,500 increase occurs because payroll taxes are being imposed on two salaries of $60,000 at the rate of 15.3 percent, rather than on one salary of $120,000 at the rates of 15.3 percent on the wage base and 2.9 percent on salary above the wage base.

Each of your corporations will also withhold social security taxes from your paycheck; but as an employee, you have to pay your share of the social security tax on the wage base only one time, and you may recover all taxes on the wage base withheld from you by the second corporation. In the previous example, since your total salary was $120,000, your total share of the social security tax would be approximately $5,600. Furthermore, because together your two corporations would have withheld $9,280 in social security taxes, you would get a refund of some $3,600. But your corporations would get no such refund; each would be charged the social security tax on the wage base at the 7.65 percent rate.

You might think that you can avoid these increased corporate social security taxes by paying yourself a salary of $120,000 from one corporation and no salary from the other corporation. But the IRS might not accept that. If you have performed valuable services for both corporations, it may charge you with salary from both corporations (so that it can collect the additional social security taxes).

Depending on your business, a possible solution to this excessive social security tax predicament is to own your corporations through a holding company that is also a management company. Your management company provides management services to your operating companies and charges them for those services. No social security taxes are imposed on payments to a management company for management services. These management services are actually performed by you as an employee of the holding company, and the holding company pays you one salary, which is subject to payroll taxes, with the funds that it receives from the operating companies. This strategy is more likely to work—though there are no guarantees—if your holding company really looks like a management company, that is, it has other employees besides you who also provide management services to your operating companies, and if your operating companies also have other officers (since every company should have its own officers).

MISTAKE 72
▶ **Having more than one corporation.**

Increased social security taxes, the need to offset profits with losses, consolidated returns, the need to have basis in an S corporation—all these factors should at the least cause you to consider whether you really need two corporations to run your different businesses. Maybe, because of the nature of your business, you do need two or more corporations, whatever the tax consequences; but many very large companies operate quite happily through several divisions of one corporation (General Motors is an example). If it's not necessary from a business standpoint, having more than one corporation is often a bad idea from a tax standpoint.

Chapter Twelve

Estate Planning for Small-Business Owners

Depending on your other assets, a business worth more than about $1.7 million could generate an estate tax of 40 percent of its value above $1.7 million when you die. A business worth more than about $2.7 million could generate a tax of 50 percent of its value above $2.7 million. The complaint that a family business has to be sold to pay the taxes is a common one, and there is no happy solution for owners of family businesses who want to pass the business on to their children. This chapter examines some of the mistakes that business owners make that exacerbate this problem.

A PRIMER IN FEDERAL ESTATE TAXATION

The federal estate tax starts at 18 percent on a "taxable estate" of $10,000 or less. It doesn't stay there very long. It climbs to 30 percent once the taxable estate exceeds $100,000, to 37 percent once the taxable estate exceeds $500,000, to 41 percent once the taxable estate exceeds $1 million, to 49 percent once the taxable estate exceeds $2 million, and tops off at 55 percent for taxable estates in excess of $3 million (there are several additional tax brackets along the way).

The Marital Deduction

As most people should realize, however, the taxable estate is not the same as the estate's value. The taxable estate is the net value of the estate (that is, the gross value of the estate, less the decedent's debts), less the value of any property left to the decedent's spouse. Therefore, if the owner of a business leaves the business to his spouse, there is no estate tax on the business at the time of the owner's death because the value of the business for estate tax purposes is reduced to zero. An estate tax will be imposed on the business once the surviving spouse dies.

The Family Business Exclusion

Starting in 1998, in determining the taxable estate, up to $700,000 of the value of a family-owned business may be excluded from the estate. A family-owned business is defined generally as a business that is at least 50 percent owned by the decedent and members of his family (or at least 70 percent owned by two families, or at least 90 percent owned by three families, as long as the decedent and his family own at least 30 percent of the business). For the exclusion to apply, (1) the value of the business must account for at least 50 percent of the value of the decedent's adjusted gross estate, (2) the decedent or members of his family must have worked in the business during at least five of the eight years preceding the decedent's death, and (3) the decedent's interest in the business must pass to members of his family or to someone who, though not a member of the family, has actively worked for the business for at least ten years before the decedent's death. Moreover, for the benefit of the exclusion to be fully enjoyed, the people who inherit the decedent's interest in the business must continue to work in the business for ten years after the decedent's death. This family business exclusion is designed to help families avoid having to sell their small businesses in order to pay estate taxes when the owner dies and when much of his estate consists of the family business. Under this family business exclusion, therefore, the owner of a family business can pass on $700,000 worth of that business free of estate tax even if he does not leave it to his spouse.

The Unified Credit

Even after the taxable estate has been determined, the estate tax is not imposed on all of it. Every estate gets an automatic credit of up to $192,800 against the amount of tax it owes. Since it takes a taxable estate of $600,000 to generate an estate tax of $192,800, it is often said that the first $600,000 of an estate is tax-free. Starting in 1998, the amount of the estate tax credit gradually increases over a period of nine years so that, by the year 2006, the first $1 million of an estate will be tax-free.

The combination of the family business exclusion and the unified credit means that a family business worth up to $1,300,000 may be left to children or other family members tax-free even if no part of the business is left to a spouse. (Although the unified credit will increase over the next several years, the portion of a family business that may be left tax-free to family members other than a spouse will remain at $1,300,000.) But remember, when you use your entire unified credit to shield your business from estate taxes, other assets in your estate not left to your spouse will themselves be subject to estate taxes.

There are, therefore, three major estate tax benefits that can be used to reduce the estate tax on your business (as well as your other assets): the marital deduction, the family business exclusion, and the unified credit. We now turn to the basic estate plan that utilizes these benefits.

MISTAKE 73
▸ **Dying with a business but without an estate plan.**

If your estate is worth about $2 million and consists mostly of a family business, and if you die with a will that simply leaves everything to your spouse and provides for no other estate plan, your estate will pay no tax upon your death, but once your spouse dies, the estate will pay a tax of about $270,000. The goal of a basic estate plan is to provide for all of your assets to pass tax-free to your children after both you and your spouse have died. Until recently, a basic estate plan could accomplish that goal only if your estate was worth $1.2 million or less, and here is how it worked:

Starting with an estate of $1.2 million, you left $600,000 of your estate to your spouse; that reduced your taxable estate to $600,000; you left the balance of your estate to your children; your estate paid no tax because the unified credit eliminated the tax on a taxable estate of $600,000. When your spouse died, assuming that she lived off the income of the $600,000 you left her and neither increased nor depleted the principal, she left her entire estate to the children; since her taxable estate was $600,000, there was no tax on her estate, either. Your children had all $1.2 million of your estate, and the government took none of it.

With the enactment of the family business exclusion, you can now presumably pass an estate worth up to $1.9 million tax-free to your children following the death of you and your spouse, provided that $700,000 of your estate consists of interests in a family business. By leaving the family business to members of the family (or longtime employees), you can reduce the value of your estate back to $1.2 million, and then apply the basic estate plan described above. (As the $600,000 exclusion increases over the next several years, you will be able to pass an even larger estate tax-free to your children.)

As tax experts study the impact of the new family business exclusion, they may design more sophisticated basic estate plans to maximize the benefits of the exclusion, but that is how a basic estate plan works.

If you are uncomfortable about leaving half your estate to your children (or to your spouse), you can use trusts to protect your heirs from themselves. You can leave the children's $600,000 in a trust that distributes the money to them when they attain a designated age; you can put your spouse's $600,000 in another trust that pays her the income for life and then passes the money to the children upon her death. But the basic estate plan is the same.

If your estate is worth $1.9 million or less and includes a family business worth no more than $700,000, that is all the estate planning you have to do in order to avoid all estate taxes (though you may wish to do additional planning for nontax purposes), and you needn't read any further. But if your estate is worth significantly more than $1.9 million, then you have your work cut out for you, particularly when your estate includes a family business worth more than $700,000.

REDUCING THE ESTATE TAX ON FAMILY BUSINESSES

If your estate is worth more than $1.9 million (assuming more than $700,000 in family interests), then estate taxes will be due unless you take one of these five actions:

1. You give away your assets in small doses that aren't subject to tax.

2. You buy insurance to pay the taxes.
3. You "freeze" the value of your assets in order to limit the damage.
4. You sell your assets before you die.
5. You give your assets to a charity.

Since you seldom see a small businessperson who wants to give his family business to a charity, we will look mostly at the first four alternatives.

MISTAKE 74
▶ **Failing to establish a small gift program.**

As most people know, you can make annual gifts of $10,000 to as many people as you like, tax-free. You can give $10,000 to your son, $10,000 to your daughter, $10,000 to your nephew, $10,000 to the mailman — as many gifts as you like of $10,000 or less, and they are all tax-free. A gift in excess of $10,000 while you are alive is taxed in exactly the same way as your estate is taxed when you die, but gifts of $10,000 or less are never taxed.

If you are married, your spouse can let you use her annual $10,000 gift-tax exemption, so you and your spouse together can make as many gifts of $20,000 as you like. All tax-free, forever.

These so-called annual gift-tax exemptions (I'll call them "small gifts") do not have to be made in cash; they can be made in property, including stock or some other interest in the family business. Over time, small gifts can be used to remove a substantial part of your business from your estate tax-free.

If your family business is run through a corporation, then in order to make small gifts, you first have to obtain an estimate of the value of your corporation. Then you have to divide up the stock of your corporation into units that permit you to make gifts of stock worth $10,000 (or $20,000 if you are married and your spouse will lend you her small-gift exemption). If your corporation were worth $2 million, you could issue 200 shares of stock with a value of $10,000 per share. Then you and your spouse could give your children two shares of stock each year. If you had two children, you could give away, tax-free, 4 percent of your company every year. It doesn't sound like much, but after ten years, you've removed 40 percent of your company from your estate and saved perhaps close to $400,000 in estate taxes.

The real tax savings come, however, as the family business increases in value. Any increase in value in the business after your children own a part of it is partly reflected in their shares. If your company doubles in value over the ten years following the completion of your small-gift program, your children now own 40 percent of a company worth $4 million. Had their stock been in your estate, it would have been subject to an estate tax of as much as $800,000. But all that stock, with all that value, is owned by your children and is not subject to estate taxes when you die.

Of course, it does not always work as perfectly as just described. Your company is more likely to increase in value as you make your small gifts, and each year $20,000 worth of your company is reflected in a smaller number of shares of stock (and, therefore, a smaller percentage of the company). Nonetheless, as the company grows in value, the value of the stock owned by your children grows with it, and that stock will not be taxed as part of your estate when you die.

Estate taxes are not the only factor to consider when making a small-gift program of stock in your company. There may be real-life factors, too. If your children own 40 percent of the company, they are entitled to 40 percent of any dividends that the company declares. This may not trouble you if you pay yourself a salary equal to the company's earnings every year so that there are no dividends. There may also be income-tax consequences. If yours is an S corporation, your children will be taxed on 40 percent of the company's taxable income. But again, this factor is of concern to you only if, after paying your salary, the company has taxable income. But in light of these consequences, a small-gift program involving stock in your business should not be undertaken without first consulting an attorney.

People who run their business through sole proprietorships can also give away a part of their business every year. When you make a gift of the first 2 percent of your sole proprietorship to your children, you will usually create a partnership (in which your children will be limited partners). Thereafter, you start giving them a percentage of your partnership interest every year. Otherwise, the plan (and the consequences) are essentially the same as when you make gifts of stock in a corporation. Again, however, consult with an attorney before you start.

The small-gift program is elemental estate tax

planning. Many people do it with cash, which is fine, but when you do it with appreciating property, the tax savings grow each year as the property appreciates in value. And it pays to start early.

MISTAKE 75
▶ Failing to fund estate tax liability with insurance.

Another way to pass on your family business to your children without giving half of it to the government is to buy life insurance that provides funds when you die to pay your estate taxes. If your estate faces a $500,000 estate tax liability, a $500,000 life insurance policy will provide the money to pay those taxes just when you need it. The important thing, however, is to make sure that the $500,000 in insurance proceeds are not also included in your estate. If they are, then your estate will have to use half the proceeds to pay the tax just on the proceeds; thus, it will come up $250,000 short in funds needed to pay the estate tax on the business.

The proceeds of a life insurance policy are included in your estate only if you own the policy when you die. So if you are buying insurance to pay estate taxes, make sure someone else owns the policy. Since the owner of a life insurance policy can change the beneficiary of the policy at any time, it's important that the owner of the policy be someone you trust—your spouse, in most instances. And, if necessary, you can make gifts to your spouse each year to enable her to pay the premiums on the insurance policy (all gifts to spouses are tax-free). When you die, your spouse collects the insurance proceeds tax-free and uses them to pay the estate taxes on your business.

If you don't trust your spouse, a trust can be established to accomplish the same purpose. The trust owns the policy, and you make annual gifts to the trust to enable it to pay the premiums on the policy. For every beneficiary of the trust, you can make a tax-free gift of $10,000. And your spouse can join you to permit a tax-free gift of $20,000. If you have two children who are the beneficiaries of the trust, you can give the trust up to $40,000 each year, which will buy you a lot of insurance. When you die, the trust collects the proceeds of the policy tax-free and distributes them to your children, who use the money to pay your estate taxes. However, trusts used for this purpose, called *irrevocable life insurance trusts*, are somewhat tricky. They cannot be drafted by a layperson, so you will need professional help with this kind of estate tax planning.

MISTAKE 76
▶ Failing to freeze the value of your estate.

An estate freeze is damage control. You've conceded that your estate is going to pay some taxes when you die; you're just trying to keep the amount of tax reasonable — and usually that means paying some tax now.

Estate freeze planning involves maintaining the value of your assets as currently calculated. The previous section described a partial use of an estate freeze plan—a small-gift program, by which each time you got another 2 percent of your business's stock out of your estate, you also eliminated from your estate the appreciation in value on that stock.

The simplest version of a complete estate freeze is to give away everything you own today. If your family business is worth $1 million, you give it to your children today, claim the unified credit to eliminate the tax on $600,000 worth of the business, and pay a gift tax of about $148,000 (the family business exclusion does not apply to lifetime gifts). It may seem like a lot of money to pay today rather than years from now, but what justifies an estate freeze is that years from now the business may be worth $4 million, and then the estate tax would be more than $1 million. Before you give away the business, you might enter into a long-term employment contract that pays you a generous salary and provides you with money for the future.

Why doesn't everybody just use the small-gift program to slowly remove a business from their estate? Many people do, if they start young enough. An estate freeze becomes necessary when you're older and you don't have enough time to remove sufficient assets from your estate. It also becomes necessary when your business is growing in value so fast that, limited to the $10,000 or $20,000 small gifts you can make each year, you could never get ahead of the game that way.

In fact, estate freezes come in a variety of complex packages, most of them beyond the scope of this book, but the following are some strategies to ask an attorney about:

- *Recapitalization of your business.* The object of a recapitalization is to create two kinds of stock, one of which increases in value more quickly than the other, then give this fast-appreciating stock to your children (with luck, at a time when it's not worth much). In the meantime, you still get to run the business (which, you may feel, is best for your children in the long run). Recapitalizations, which once were quite popular but now are severely restricted by the tax laws, are very complex, but they may still be useful to some people in some situations.

- *Grantor-retained annuity trusts.* In a grantor-retained annuity trust, you put assets into a trust and retain the right to receive an annuity from the trust for a number years. The remaindermen of the trust — your children — get whatever remains in the trust after the annuity term expires. To avoid paying a gift tax on the value of the "remainder" interest promised to your children, you choose an annuity term and an annuity rate (which cannot be below an IRS-determined rate), which, based on the value of the assets placed in trust, would exhaust the trust by the time the annuity ends. If the assets don't appreciate in value, the trust will in fact be exhausted at the end of the annuity, and you will have accomplished nothing (you won't have lost anything, either). But if those assets do appreciate in value, the trust will still have funds once the annuity ends, and your children get those funds at a low or zero tax cost. With careful (and difficult) planning, some family business stock can be used to fund a grantor-retained annuity trust.

- *Playing with valuations.* The lower you can value a gift of a family business interest, the less you will pay in gift tax when you embark on your estate freeze — and sometimes there are ways to reduce the value of the gift that you make. Taking advantage of "minority discounts" is one way. A gift of less than 50 percent of the stock of a family business is worth less per share of stock than a gift of a controlling interest (because theoretically no one would pay full value for a minority interest in a closely held corporation). The timing of a gift can also affect its value. If you give away a portion of your company during a low period in your industry, the business may be worth less than it will be in a few years after the industry has recovered.

Selling Your Business Before You Die

Selling your business — to your children, of course — is another way to freeze the value of your business in your estate.

If you sell your business today at its fair market value of $1 million, and it grows to a value of $3 million by the time you die, you have saved about $500,000 in estate tax. This savings assumes that when you die you still have the $1 million that your children paid for the business. If you've spent it, the savings will be greater. How do your children pay for the business? One way to help them do so is to make an installment sale so that they can pay for it over time — perhaps out of the earnings of the business or with small gifts that you make to them each year. Just because you sell your business doesn't mean that you can't keep working for it — you can, and for a generous salary, too.

It would take more than the whole of this book to examine estate freezing techniques in detail. They are practically an area of tax law unto themselves. But if you have a rapidly growing business — it should already be worth several million dollars for an estate freeze plan to be worthwhile — estate freezes may be worth considering.

Afterword

The seventy-six mistakes covered in this book are not hypothetical scenarios that might disrupt your business. None is anything out of the ordinary; none is made up. Each actually occurs and, more important, occurs on a more-or-less regular basis. Tax advisers see them over and over again. Indeed, as I was preparing this afterword, a very successful businessperson reported to his attorney that his S corporation had recently admitted as a shareholder another corporation formed by two people who wanted to invest in his business. Any problem there? Indeed there was, he was told, but a problem that, if attended to promptly, could be undone — by collapsing the investing corporation so that the investors owned stock directly in his company, and by writing a very apologetic letter to the IRS. No problem, the businessman replied; he would attend to that forthwith. Then his attorney asked him one more question: Were these individuals both U.S. citizens or residents? "No," he said, "They're French. They live in Paris. Is *that* a problem?"

And so it goes. Businesspeople, understandably more interested in their businesses than in the government's out-of-left-field regulations, march right into the traps that the tax laws have set. The businessperson with the doubly disqualified S corporation simply wanted new investors in his business; he couldn't have cared less how they chose to invest in his company, what nationality they were, or where they lived. But the mistake, had it gone undetected or uncorrected, would have increased his company's tax bill by at least 35 percent — and the best lawyer in the world couldn't have helped him.

Regrettably, problems like these confront all businesspeople. I hope that the seventy-six mistakes I have covered here will help you to avoid many of them. But because no book can cover all such mistakes, I also hope that this book has raised your consciousness level and has made you aware that you operate your business in what, at least where taxes are concerned, is often an Alice-in-Wonderland world. Almost every time you do something significant in your business, you must ask the question: Are there tax ramifications? If you don't know the answer, you should assume that there are tax consequences, usually bad ones, then promptly consult someone who does know the answer.

Index

above-the-line deductions,
45–47
accident insurance, tax-free,
130
accountable plan
business connection
requirement, 46–51
definition, 46
per diem reimburse-
ments, 60, 62–63
return requirement, 58–
60, 63
substantiation
requirement, 51–58, 60,
62–63
written, need for, 63–64
accumulated earnings tax,
34–36
annual gift-tax exemption
gifts, 150, 151–154
Annual Lease Value,
automobile, 73–74
annuity trusts, grantor-
retained, 157–158
athletic facilities, on-
premises, 66
automobiles
cents-per-mile rule, 75–76
lease valuation rule, 73–74

reimbursement of
expenses, 56–58
as working condition
fringe benefits, 69–70,
73–76

bank accounts, separate,
98–99
bank loans. *See also*
business loans;
personal loans
payroll taxes not remitted
by bank, 9–10
to S corporations, 126–
127
bonuses, 30, 33, 71–72
burden of proof, 30
business connection
requirement, 46–51
business expenses, 29. *See
also* entertainment
expenses; travel
expenses
bona fide expenses *vs.*
nonbusiness expenses,
47–50
listed property, 56–58
wages, treated as (*See
wages*)

163

business interest, deduction of, 88–92
business loans
  for investment purposes, 90–91
  partnerships, money borrowed by owner for, 101
  pension plan, to or from, 114–115
  for personal use, 91–92
  S corporations, money borrowed by owner for, 100–101
  separate bank accounts for, 98–99
  tracing rules, 93–100
business purpose of expenses
  entertainment, 55–56
  listed property, 57
  per diem reimbursements, 63
  travel, 53, 63
business purpose of fringe benefits, 71, 73

capital contribution to company, 43, 126–127
cars. *See* automobiles
cents-per-mile rule, use of, 75–76
children, estate planning for. *See* estate planning
client meeting home office deduction, 79–80

collateral, for loan, 38
comparable salaries, 32
computers
  expenses reimbursed for, 56–58
  as fringe benefit, 69–70, 71
consolidated tax return, 136–138, 140
convenience of employer home office deduction test, 81–82
corporation
  authorization of loan by resolution of, 38
  deductions by, 29, 30, 43
  loan treatment on books of, 37–38
  loans to/from owners (*See* loans)
  owner(s)' personal liability for payroll tax payments, 6–12
  as S corporation shareholders, 121
  S corporations compared, 132–133
  taxes paid by, 28–30, 34–36, 41
court challenges
  burden of proof, 30
  independent contractor *vs.* employee, 23
  reasonable compensation claim, 30
credit card, use of, 51